NEW DIRECTIONS FOR COMMUNITY COLLEGES

Arthur M. Cohen
EDITOR-IN-CHIEF

Florence B. Brawer
ASSOCIATE EDITOR

Paula Zeszotarski
PUBLICATION COORDINATOR

Beyond Access: Methods and Models for Increasing Retention and Learning Among Minority Students

Steven R. Aragon
University of Illinois at Urbana-Champaign

EDITOR

D1560350

Number 112, Winter 2000

JOSSEY-BASS
San Francisco

ERIC®

Clearinghouse for Community Colleges

BEYOND ACCESS: METHODS AND MODELS FOR INCREASING RETENTION AND LEARNING AMONG
MINORITY STUDENTS
Steven R. Aragon (ed.)
New Directions for Community Colleges, no. 112
Volume XXVIII, number 4
Arthur M. Cohen, Editor-in-Chief
Florence B. Brawer, Associate Editor

New Directions for Community Colleges is indexed in Current Index to Journals in Education (ERIC).

Microfilm copies of issues and articles are available in 16mm and 35mm, as well as microfiche in
105mm, through University Microfilms Inc., 300 North Zeeb Road, Ann Arbor, Michigan 48106-
1346.

ISSN 0194-3081   ISBN 0-7879-5429-2

NEW DIRECTIONS FOR COMMUNITY COLLEGES is part of The Jossey-Bass Higher and Adult Education
Series and is published quarterly by Jossey-Bass Inc., 350 Sansome Street, San Francisco, California 94104-1342, in association with the ERIC Clearinghouse for Community Colleges. Periodicals
postage paid at San Francisco, California, and at additional mailing offices. POSTMASTER: Send
address changes to New Directions for Community Colleges, Jossey-Bass Inc., 350 Sansome Street,
San Francisco, California 94104-1342.

SUBSCRIPTIONS cost $60.00 for individuals and $107.00 for institutions, agencies, and libraries.
Prices subject to change.

THE MATERIAL in this publication is based on work sponsored wholly or in part by the Office of Educational Research and Improvement, U.S. Department of Education, under contract number ED-
99-CO-0010. Its contents do not necessarily reflect the views of the Department or any other agency
of the U.S. Government.

EDITORIAL CORRESPONDENCE should be sent to the Editor-in-Chief, Arthur M. Cohen, at the ERIC
Clearinghouse for Community Colleges, University of California, 3051 Moore Hall, Box 951521,
Los Angeles, California 90095-1521. All manuscripts receive anonymous reviews by external ref-
erees.

Cover photograph © Rene Sheret, After Image, Los Angeles, California, 1990.

Printed in the United States of America on acid-free recycled paper containing 100 percent recov-
ered waste paper, of which at least 20 percent is postconsumer waste

CONTENTS

EDITOR'S NOTES

Although in recent years the status of people of color has improved, there is still considerable evidence that U.S. society is battling problems of racism and sexism and is very stratified on the basis of race, gender, and disability. "In fact, stratification based on socioeconomic status is a prominent feature of U.S. society, and social policy in the last four decades has made little sustained attempt to change it" (Sleeter and Grant, 1999, p. 2). People of color continue to experience poverty and unemployment disproportionately. According to 1995 U.S. Bureau of the Census data (as reported by Sleeter and Grant), whites reported unemployment rates of 5.3 percent, Hispanics 9.9 percent, and African Americans 11.5 percent. While these data are not reported as systematically for American Indians, the unemployment rate has averaged 27.5 percent and has been reported to be as high as 52.4 percent for the Navajo tribe. As a result of differential access to jobs, housing, and health services, other estimates related to quality of life vary by ethnicity (Sleeter and Grant). For example, white Americans are more likely to be covered by health insurance than are African Americans and Hispanic Americans. Whites also enjoy a longer life expectancy than Americans of color and are less likely to be imprisoned. In addition, people of color are still locked out of much of the political system, even though increasing numbers of big-city mayors are people of color. Readers of these data should keep in mind that while there are similarities between each of these minority groups, there are barriers and issues that are unique to each group.

Although the last four decades may have brought improved social status and access to education for ethnic minorities, African Americans, Hispanics, Asians/Pacific Islanders, and American Indians/Alaska Natives are still disenfranchised. According to researchers, minority students are considered more likely than their white counterparts to be at risk of academic failure at the elementary, secondary, and postsecondary levels (O'Brien and Zudak, 1998; Rendon and Hope, 1996). The risk factors associated with not completing a postsecondary program include delayed enrollment, part-time attendance, being self-supporting, single-parent status, a full-time work schedule, caring for a dependent, and holding a GED certificate. According to a National Postsecondary Student Aid Study (as reported by O'Brien and Zudak), 27 percent of Hispanic students, 31 percent of African American students, and 35 percent of American Indian/Alaska Native students have four or more of these risk factors, compared with 22 percent of white students. Another potential risk for minority students is that they may be trying to break new ground as the first in their families to attend college (O'Brien and Zudak). While these data represent the averages for the different groups of students, readers need to realize that enormous diversity exists within these four populations.

Minority Students' Access to Community Colleges: The Current Picture

The demographic projections for the next decade call for dramatic theoretical, conceptual, and practical paradigm shifts within the teaching and learning arena. Today, racial and ethnic minorities make up about 28 percent of the U.S. population (U.S. Bureau of the Census, 1998). According to the U.S. Bureau of the Census (1996) projections, by 2050, minorities will make up about 47 percent of the U.S. population.

Students of color account for almost one-quarter (24.8 percent) of postsecondary education enrollment, with African Americans representing approximately 12 percent, Hispanics 9 percent, Asians/Pacific Islanders 3 percent, and American Indians/Alaska Natives .8 percent (O'Brien and Zudak, 1998). During the period between 1976 and 1994, postsecondary enrollment increased nearly 30 percent, with minority students accounting for more than half of this gain. Consequently, the term *minority* is losing its statistical meaning, as a new student majority rapidly emerges, comprising, collectively, African Americans, Hispanics/Latinos, Asians/Pacific Islanders, and American Indians/Alaska Natives (Rendon and Hope, 1996).

In American higher education, community colleges play a significant role in providing educational access and opportunity to a diverse student population. Each fall, approximately half of all minority undergraduates enrolled in higher education attend a community college. Arguably, community college campuses reflect the diversity of the American population. Enrolled students are of all ages and come from different cultural and ethnic backgrounds. In fact, among minorities, community colleges are the schools of choice (American Association of Community Colleges, 1998).

According to the American Association of Community Colleges (2000), these institutions saw an increase in enrollments of minority students between 1992 and 1997. There were only slight enrollment increases for American Indians/Alaska Natives (from 1.1 percent in 1992 to 1.3 percent in 1997) and Asians/Pacific Islanders (from 5.0 percent in 1992 to 5.8 percent in 1997) attending community colleges during these years. However, community colleges saw slightly higher enrollment rates for African Americans (from 9.9 percent in 1992 to 11.1 percent in 1997) and Hispanics (from 9.3 percent in 1992 to 11.8 percent in 1997) during this period.

Although minority students (24.9 percent) still lag behind white students (31.4 percent) in attaining a high school degree, this gap is beginning to narrow, especially for African American and American Indian students. This suggests that their future enrollment in community colleges will continue to increase (see Table 3.1 in American Association of Community College's *National Profile of Community Colleges*, 2000).

Student success among minority students at community colleges is also on the rise. Since the late 1980s, students of color have earned increasing numbers of degrees (American Council on Education, 2000). Although the rate of growth has varied considerably among the four major ethnic minority groups, each group has made gains at every degree level. Since 1987, minority students have outpaced white students in their rate of increase at all degree levels.

Students of color accounted for 22.8 percent of all associate degree recipients in 1997—the third consecutive year they have earned more than 20 percent of all associate degrees (American Council on Education, 2000). African American students represented 9 percent of these graduates, Hispanic students 7 percent, Asian/Pacific Islander students 5 percent, and American Indian/Alaska Native students 1 percent (American Association of Community Colleges, 2000). This 22.8 percent rate in 1997 was up more than 1 percentage point from 1996, more than 4 percentage points from 1993, and nearly 7 percentage points from 1987. But compared with their share of two-year college enrollments (31.3 percent in 1997), students of color remain underrepresented in degree awards. Despite increased access and success achieved by students of color, challenges remain.

Although the open-door accessibility of community colleges has played a critical role in the process of upward mobility in American society, the question of whether community colleges enhance the social mobility of working-class and minority students remains in question (Shaw, Rhoads, and Valadez, 1999). Community colleges have been criticized for failing to acknowledge or adapt to the diversity in their student populations, resulting in low transfer rates and consistently high dropout rates.

The Current Challenge: Improving the Learning Environment

In view of current demographic realities, fostering student success in educational environments for students of various cultures and socioeconomic backgrounds requires institutions to rethink their curricula, testing practices, methods of instruction, counseling techniques, and delivery systems of other specific services (Clark and Waltzman, 1993; Dunn and Griggs, 1995). This shift to a more diverse student population also presents a challenge for the faculty. According to Clark and Cheng (1993), "in order to effectively educate all student groups, faculty will need to achieve cultural literacy and cross-cultural communicative competency" (p. 5).

A large part of this challenge is for educators to become more competent in the knowledge, skills, abilities, and attitudes that can lead to higher retention and learning success for these students (Clark and Cheng, 1993; Wlodkowski, 1999; Wlodkowski and Ginsberg, 1995). As differences in language, cultural values, principles, and practices become more vivid in today's classrooms, educational programs will need broader curricula that include multicultural and multilinguistic information. Brookfield (1996, p. 379) probably states it best when he says that "it is necessary to challenge the ethnocentrism of much theorizing . . . which assumes that adult learning . . . is synonymous with the learning undertaken in university continuing education classes by White American middle-class adults in the postwar era."

The implications of not better understanding and addressing the learning needs of our minority students for society in general and adult education in particular are staggering. Briscoe and Ross (1989) stress the urgency of the problem: "It is likely that young people will leave school early, will never participate fully in society or in the decision-making processes of government, and that they will neither enjoy the benefits of good health, nor experience the upward mobility needed as adults to make them full contributors and partners in shaping and participating in the larger society" (p. 586). A decade later, these concerns have not yet been resolved (O'Brien and Zudak, 1998; Rendon and Hope, 1996).

Increasing Retention and Learning Success for Minority Students

The purpose of education is to help younger and older adults become better citizens of society and prepare them for the world of work. Society and work do not cater to one type of working or learning style. Consequently, all students need to be prepared to approach learning from a holistic perspective, using skills and abilities that may be outside their comfort zones. By taking a holistic approach, faculty and administrators help students strengthen their current abilities as well as develop additional ones.

The purpose of this volume is to offer community college educators alternative models, approaches, and perspectives to consider in working with students of color. The volume begins with an analysis of how community colleges assess their students for admission and placement. Current research supports the idea that minority students do not perform well on many of the traditional evaluation and assessment measures commonly used in community college classrooms. In Chapter One, Romero Jalomo reviews alternative ways of measuring student performance and provides strategies for helping students perform better on the traditional measures.

Students' educational and career goals influence their performance in, and expectations of, the classroom. Research has found that minority students have different educational and career goals in relation to their white counterparts. These goals influence how they approach their educational experiences. In Chapter Two, Frankie Santos Laanan identifies these perceptions and discusses how educators can take them into account when designing and developing educational programs.

In Chapter Three, Irene M. Sanchez presents a theoretical model for measuring student learning style that takes a holistic perspective. Historically, learning style theories have only examined learning from a cognitive perspective. This chapter addresses two additional components that should be considered.

Chapter Four offers a model by which student success courses can be designed and implemented within the community college setting. Success courses are designed to develop learning and study skills for incoming students. Martina Stovall's research has found that success courses can increase rates of persistence and completion for entering minority students.

Social learning theory can contribute significantly to the retention and learning success of minority students. In Chapter Five, Linda K. Stromei discusses the success of mentoring programs to aid in smoother transitions into the postsecondary learning environment as well as long-term retention for students of color.

In Chapter Six, Evelyn Clements presents a case study that describes one college's efforts to create respect for cultural diversity. Wide-ranging student activity planning contributed to a more inclusive campus climate and increased retention for minority students.

Technology is becoming an essential part of delivering quality education in all settings. The use of technology not only facilitates learning in the classroom but can also provide educational access to students at a distance. In Chapter Seven, Nilda Palma-Rivas discusses some of the latest technologies that are practical for use in community college classrooms. In addition, Palma-Rivas describes some of the strategies that educators should consider when incorporating educational technology into activities or complete programs.

In Chapter Eight, Barbara K. Townsend examines ways in which nonminority instructors can be better integrated into the minority learning environment. Many colleges serving minorities are still highly dependent on nonminority instructors. To be successful, these instructors must achieve cross-cultural competency. This chapter describes some of the challenges that nonminority faculty members may encounter as well as some strategies for increasing effectiveness.

Finally, Eboni M. Zamani, in Chapter Nine, reviews recent ERIC documents that highlight issues and concerns regarding minority student retention and learning success within community colleges. Zamani discusses factors contributing to declining retention rates and effective programming strategies designed to address continued participation of students of color.

In conclusion, educational institutions should view diverse student bodies as assets. Through diversity, learning experiences for both students and faculty are enriched, leading to broader perspectives and promoting flexibility in thinking. These contributions should be sought after and valued. It is my hope that the ideas and models presented by the authors in the following chapters will open up new ways of thinking for achieving this goal.

Steven R. Aragon
Editor

References

American Association of Community Colleges. *Pocket Profile of Community Colleges: Trends and Statistics 1997–1998*. Washington, D.C.: Community College Press, 1998.

American Association of Community Colleges. *National Profile of Community Colleges: Trends and Statistics*. (3rd ed.) Washington, D.C.: Community College Press, 2000.

American Council on Education. *Minorities in Higher Education 1999–2000*. Washington, D.C.: American Council on Education, 2000.

Briscoe, D. B., and Ross, J. M. "Racial and Ethnic Minorities and Adult Education." In S. B. Merriam and P. M. Cunningham (eds.), *Handbook of Adult and Continuing Education*. San Francisco: Jossey-Bass, 1989, pp. 583–598.

Brookfield, S. D. "Adult Learning: An Overview." In A. C. Tuijnman (ed.), International Encyclopedia of Adult Education and Training. (2nd ed.) New York: Pergamon Press, 1996.

Clark, L. W., and Cheng, L. L. "Faculty Challenges in Facing Diversity." In L. W. Clark and D. E. Waltzman (eds.), *Faculty and Student Challenges in Facing Cultural and Linguistic Diversity*. Springfield, Ill.: Thomas, 1993, pp. 5–24.

Clark, L. W., and Waltzman, D. E. (eds.). *Faculty and Student Challenges in Facing Cultural and Linguistic Diversity*. Springfield, Ill.: Thomas, 1993.

Dunn, R., and Griggs, S. A. *Multiculturalism and Learning Style: Teaching and Counseling Adolescents*. New York: Praeger, 1995.

O'Brien, E. M., and Zudak, C. "Minority-Serving Institutions: An Overview." In J. P. Merisotis and C. T. O'Brien (eds.), *Minority-Serving Institutions: Distinct Purposes, Common Goals*. San Francisco: Jossey-Bass, 1998, pp. 5–15.

Rendon, L. I., and Hope, R. O. "An Educational System in Crisis." In L. I. Rendon and R. O. Hope (eds.), *Educating a New Majority: Transforming America's Educational System for Diversity*. San Francisco: Jossey-Bass, 1996, pp. 1–32.

Shaw, K. M., Rhoads, R. A., and Valadez, J. R. "Community Colleges as Cultural Texts: A Conceptual Overview." In K. M. Shaw, J. R. Valadez, and R. A. Rhoads (eds.), *Community Colleges as Cultural Texts: Qualitative Explorations of Organizational and Student Culture*. Albany, N.Y.: State University of New York Press, 1999, pp. 1–13.

Sleeter, C. E., and Grant, C. A. *Making Choices for Multicultural Education: Five Approaches to Race, Class, and Gender* (3rd ed.). New York: Wiley, 1999.

U.S. Bureau of the Census. *Current Population Reports*. Washington, D.C.: U.S. Department of Commerce, 1996, p. 1.

U.S. Bureau of the Census. *Age, Sex, Race, and Hispanic Origin Reports*. Washington, D.C.: U.S. Department of Commerce, 1998, pp. 2–3.

Wlodkowski, R. J. *Enhancing Adult Motivation to Learn: A Comprehensive Guide for Teaching All Adults*. San Francisco: Jossey-Bass, 1999.

Wlodkowski, R. J., and Ginsberg, M. B. *Diversity and Motivation: Culturally Responsive Teaching*. San Francisco: Jossey-Bass, 1995.

STEVEN R. ARAGON *is assistant professor of community college leadership at the University of Illinois at Urbana-Champaign.*

1

Recent studies suggest that minority students do not perform well on standardized assessment measures commonly used to evaluate their preparation for and performance in college. This chapter examines student outcomes and criticisms surrounding standardized achievement testing and discusses strategies for employing alternative assessment approaches.

Assessing Minority Student Performance

Romero Jalomo Jr.

Reports on minority student preparation for and performance in college continue to yield contradictory results. While today's minority students appear better prepared for college success than the generation that preceded them, their performance on achievement tests and persistence in college leaves cause for concern. Despite inconclusive findings, minority student outcomes continue to draw the attention of external constituencies (accreditation organizations, state and local legislators, district boards, taxpayers, and parents) and internal constituencies (administrators, faculty members, institutional researchers, counseling staff members, and academic advisors) who function as stakeholders in an era of higher education accountability (Cress, 1996). Today's colleges and universities enroll a more diverse student population in terms of demographic makeup, learning styles, and academic preparation than at any other time in American history (Jalomo, 2000; Terenzini and others, 1996). However, colleges and universities remain under the watchful eye of multiple stakeholder groups to ensure their efficiency and effectiveness in delivering quality instruction.

In an era of public debate and scrutiny concerning college access, educators are challenged to provide meaningful, substantive, and conducive learning experiences to a diverse population of students. In addition, the challenge remains to select and administer appropriate measures to assess their preparation for college, skills acquisition, and college outcomes. This chapter examines how traditional assessment measures of minority student preparation for and performance in college have produced differential results, and offers suggestions for alternative approaches to measuring skills acquisition in the college environment.

Minority Student Performance on the Scholastic Achievement Test

Successful student performance on precollege achievement tests remains a vital step in gaining access to postsecondary education (House and Keeley, 1997). Over the past ten years, the number of minority students completing the Scholastic Achievement Test (SAT) has steadily increased from 25 percent (275,000) of the 1.1 million students who took the exam in 1989, to 33 percent (400,000) of the 1.2 million test takers in 1999 (Roach, 1999). Although there has been an increase in the number of minority students participating in postsecondary education, statistics reveal that, with the exception of Asian students, most are not performing at rates comparable to those of white students.

From 1986 to 1996, SAT scores for all minority groups rose slightly, with Asian students posting the largest gains (Chenoweth, 1996). In 1995, the National Center for Education Statistics reported that the percentage of college-bound seniors nationwide that attained SAT scores of 1100 or more was higher for Asian and white students than for Hispanic, African American, and American Indian students (U.S. Department of Education, 1998). Yet Lederman (1998) reported that the gap in SAT scores between African American and white students recorded between 1976 and 1998 consistently averaged more than 200 points. In addition, House and Keeley (1997) reported that American Indian SAT scores were still, on average, lower than white student scores and that American Indians were less likely than white students to achieve SAT scores high enough for them to be considered for admission to selective universities.

Overall, the gap between blacks and whites has narrowed, from a 260-point difference in 1976 to a 201-point difference in 1999 (Owen and Doer, 1999). Despite overall minority student performance trailing white student scores on the SAT, the difference between minority student scores and those of white students appears to be narrowing. Although there has been some improvement among minority test scores, the overall improvement is marginal. In addition, research has demonstrated that a score gap exists across socioeconomic levels and geographic comparisons, with students from lower socioeconomic backgrounds and students from rural areas generally scoring lower (Corwin, 2000).

Criticism Surrounding Standardized Achievement Testing

Minority student performance on standardized achievement tests has inspired significant debate during the past decade. Yet during the same period, numerous studies have attempted to explain the cause of test score variance among aspiring college students. Critics argue that standardized tests are more a measure of cultural assimilation than aptitude and that they discriminate against certain student groups, namely minority students (Armstrong, Barnes, and Takabata, 1991). The SAT is perhaps the most controversial and disputed of all standardized tests used to gauge students' preparedness for later success in college.

The role of the SAT in American society is far-reaching. Each year, college-bound high school students spend millions of dollars on test preparation materials and courses. Meanwhile, real estate agents employ recent SAT averages of nearby high schools to convince families to purchase more expensive homes in exclusive neighborhoods (Chenoweth, 1997).

Because standardized achievement tests such as the SAT are used to determine scholarship eligibility in addition to college admissions decisions, the importance of addressing student performance on the examination, especially for minority students, is vital. For example, the National Merit Scholarship uses only a student's score on the Preliminary Scholastic Achievement Test (PSAT) as a qualifier. In addition, many colleges often match National Merit Scholarships with campus financial aid, resulting in full tuition awards for high PSAT scorers.

A recent U.S. Department of Education study found that one-third of students who scored 1100 or higher on the SAT were from high-income brackets whereas only 10 percent came from a low-income family. Students from high socioeconomic backgrounds were twice as likely as their middle-class counterparts to score at that level and four times as likely to score that high as students from lower socioeconomic backgrounds (Sacks, 1999). The correlation between SAT scores and socioeconomic background provides critics with an argument that suggests that the test is more a measure of parents' income and education than true student academic achievement. Nicknamed the "Volvo Effect" by Sacks (1999), these test results indicate that students from a higher socioeconomic class are more likely than those from less privileged backgrounds to achieve a high score on the SAT.

Test validity is an ongoing concern among external stakeholders who focus on minority student results on standardized achievement tests. Stakeholders in this group, ranging from legislators to educators, argue that class bias can exist in the construction of these exams. A source of contention is whether standardized assessment tests employ valid measures and accurately assess what they are supposed to measure. For instance, Murray (1998) noted that when measuring the SAT scores of white and black students in the same income range, overall scores were similar. The researcher argued that being able to comprehend a reading selection might depend more on the background and cultural experiences available to upper- or middle-class students who partake in foreign travel than on those of students from lower socioeconomic backgrounds, whose opportunities to engage in such experiences are limited.

When standardized tests are used as a major consideration in establishing admissions decisions, they can misclassify students whose educational preparation and life experiences cannot be adequately measured by forced choice examinations. Murray (1998) argues that sufficient research findings demonstrate that standardized achievement tests do not have a reliable predictability value in terms of how students will perform in the college classroom and that these tests underestimate the future grade point averages of women and minorities. Yet colleges continue to employ the SAT because they claim that it, in combination with high school grades, is a valid predictor of college performance. However, the College Board (1999) recently reported that SAT scores correlated with college grades for only 42 percent of student test takers. In contrast, high school grades were found to correlate with college grades over 48 percent of the time (Chenoweth, 1997).

Minority Student Academic Preparedness and College Persistence

In 1997, minority students represented over 26 percent of all enrolled college students in undergraduate and graduate programs in the United States (Carlson, 1999). Yet numerous studies reveal that minority students, with the exception of Asian Americans, lag behind white students in persistence and graduation rates. Recent studies suggest that a possible cause for this outcome involves student academic preparedness before enrolling in college. Astin, Tsui, and Avalos (1996) found that the most academically prepared high school students graduated from college at higher rates and often in less than five years. In their study, the researchers reported that 19.4 percent of African Americans graduated from college in four years, compared with 22.9 percent of American Indians, 26.8 percent of Puerto Ricans, 30.5 percent of Mexican Americans, 42.7 percent of whites, and 50.2 percent of Asian Americans.

When analyzing college graduation rates, Astin, Tsui, and Avalos (1996) combined SAT scores with high school grades and discovered distinct differences in time toward degree completion between highly prepared and less prepared high school graduates. The study revealed that 80.4 percent of high school graduates with an SAT score of 1300, who had an A or A+ grade point average in high school, graduated from college in four years. Conversely, only 10.5 percent of high school graduates with an overall grade point average of C or lower and SAT scores of 700 or less graduated from college in four years.

Analyzing student preparedness before college is but one of several approaches employed to better understand student performance in college. Another approach involves assessing students after their completion of general education coursework. In a national study of college student achievement, Osterlind (1997) analyzed student performance on the Basic Academic Subjects Examination (BASE), an achievement test that attempts to measure student academic skills after the completion of general education coursework. The BASE test measured student performance in four subject areas: English, mathematics, science, and social studies. Osterlind analyzed the BASE scores of 74,535 college students who completed the exam between 1988 and 1993. The researcher found that white students scored higher in reading and writing than any other student group. However, he suggested that language facility and cultural differences may account for variation in English scores between white and minority students, and that the most likely cause of score variations are the discrepancies in elementary and secondary schooling that exist between all students.

Osterlind (1997) reported that minority student scores (with the exception of those for Asian students) in the mathematics portion of the BASE exam were lower than those of white students. The researcher noted that inferior elementary and secondary schooling, combined with inadequate developmental education services, could be influential factors in student performance in mathematics. Nonetheless, there remain other explanations for minority student performance on the mathematics portion of the BASE examination that relate to test construction and test taking behaviors that may more completely account for their current BASE performance levels. For instance, the researcher concluded that white students were at a slight advantage in the math component where most of the questions were written as story problems. Furthermore, in areas where there was only computation involved, Asian students significantly outperformed all other students.

Rationale for Employing Alternative Assessment Measures

It is important for colleges to take proactive steps to identify and implement alternatives to traditional forms of assessment, especially in the areas of admissions, course placement, and persistence. Growing numbers of universities, such as the University of California and the University of Texas, as well as independent and even private colleges, are no longer employing standardized test scores as the sole or main consideration for admissions decisions. In reality, over three hundred colleges and universities no longer rely on SAT scores to solely influence their admissions decisions (Murray, 1998). Institutions such as the College of Franklin and Marshall, Bowdoin, Dickinson, and Lafayette have all reported increased student diversity from not having employed SAT scores to determine admissions eligibility. In an attempt to use alternative measures to assess student preparation for later success in college, numerous campuses have begun analyzing high school course-taking patterns and grades as a starting point. They have also required the completion of college admissions essays, interviews, and work portfolios that provide insights about a student that standardized tests cannot reveal (Murray, 1998).

Murray noted that Bates College in Maine has stopped requiring the Scholastic Achievement Test as a mechanism to assess student eligibility for college admission. Bates did so because admissions officers began to notice that as the average SAT scores required for admission rose, the number of academically talented students with low SAT scores who were deterred from applying to Bates also rose. Many of these students were members of under-represented groups such as minorities or students from nearby rural areas. The results of removing the SAT scores from admissions decisions created a more diversified student body without compromising academic quality. More important, Bates found almost no differences in the overall quality of grades earned when comparing students who had submitted SAT scores with those who had not. According to Bates College president William Hiss, "standardized scores are far less meaningful than evidence of real intelligence, real drive, real creative abilities, [or] real cultural sensitivities" (Murray, 1998, p. 36).

Alternative assessment techniques can be combined with traditional assessment methods to paint a more complete picture of a student's learning capability. In support of employing alternative assessment measures in college, Barnett (1995) argued that although test scores and academic coursework are important, other performance-based evaluations are needed to complement traditional measures. The researcher argued that assessment tests should include an active demonstration of competencies rather than a mere recitation of facts or performance of computations. In addition, Rendon (1994) noted that assessment measures that only focus on learning outcomes, as opposed to explorations into learning processes, miss the mark of gauging true student growth in college. To address these concerns, educators must recognize diverse learning styles and apply alternative assessment measures to evaluate learning for a diverse college student population effectively.

Alternatives to Assessing Student Performance in College

Alternative assessment measures to evaluate minority student performance in college can be used in combination with or in place of traditional assessment methods to develop a more comprehensive understanding of a student's learning capability and growth potential. Four alternative measures described in this section include student self-assessment, personal and social growth assessment, student portfolios, and value-added assessments. Each approach distinctly addresses aspects of student academic and noncognitive performance over a period of time. In addition, the "value-added" approach to measuring student outcomes can help educators better determine the growth that takes place in students' learning, from their enrollment in college through the completion of their undergraduate coursework.

College Student Self-Assessment. Student self-assessment is an alternative to traditional forms of achievement testing in college. Kiger (1994) noted that self-assessment provides students with the opportunity to observe and judge their own performance on a particular project or assignment. Student self-assessment also provides a nontraditional approach to evaluating student performance that avoids simply focusing on subject matter or content while offering students an opportunity to evaluate and express their individual learning preferences. The researcher argued that self-assessment can assist educators on two levels: (1) from a student perspective, it can provide information about student perceptions of learning outcomes, which can help in developmental growth, and (2) from an institutional perspective, it can help educators to determine if they are meeting stated programmatic goals by providing insight into students' expectations, development, and noncognitive growth.

Kiger's study (1994) of graduates of one community college attempted to determine whether student self-assessment was effective after the campus had incorporated general education requirements into its technical curriculum. The researcher noted that graduates reported improvement on each general education competency while acknowledging the importance of continuing education and indicating personal development and growth in professional ethics. These findings proved significant because of the demonstrated validity of student self-assessment as a measure of noncognitive growth derived from student experiences inside and outside of the classroom. The self-assessment process provided graduates with a chance to reflect on and evaluate their college experience as a whole. Kiger noted that reflection and evaluation in the self-assessment process can lead to developmental growth for students who become aware of their general education achievement, as well as motivate students to reflect on their educational experience.

The study's findings derived from student self-assessments indicated that the college generally had been successful in incorporating general education into its technical curriculum. The overall consistency of positive student self-assessments demonstrated the effectiveness of employing this type of measure to evaluate whether a campus initiative was successful in meeting its goal, while incorporating valuable input from its primary constituency—its students.

Measuring Personal and Social Growth in College. Another method of alternative assessment relates to measuring the personal development that takes place in college, determining whether students can become productive members of society, and addressing such societal issues as poverty, crime, economic development, and diversity. Graham and Cockriel (1996) studied the personal and social growth of college students and examined the effect of attending college on the overall growth process. Data were collected from 15,656 college students attending seventy-five public, private, technical, two-year, and four-year colleges and universities in the United States. Students who participated in the study had completed one or more years of college coursework.

The measure of student growth was developed by the American College Testing (ACT) program's College Outcome Survey (COS). The COS evaluated college student experiences and examined what students thought about their growth both inside and outside of the classroom (Graham and Cockriel, 1996). One section of the COS addressed student demographic information, college outcomes, student satisfaction in college, and college experiences.

The study found that students reported significant growth in academic competence, general education outcomes, responsibility, intellectual curiosity, long-term goal establishment, and self-confidence (Graham and Cockriel, 1996). The study's findings demonstrated that college gains were related to increased responsibility, goal setting, and self-confidence.

Academic self-concept is another important indicator of student success in college (Gerardi, 1990). Academic self-concept is defined as how students perceive their own academic ability and their ability to perform. Gerardi examined academic self-concept as an indicator of academic success among 98 first-year minority and low-income students at the City University of New York (CUNY) in 1987. The researcher found that academic self-concept, rather than the traditional cognitive skills as measured by the SAT and placement examinations, was a better predictor of academic success among students in programs of engineering technology.

The need for college students to develop academic self-confidence is vital to their persistence and educational goal attainment. For those students who may have limited academic success in high school, experiencing success in college can help build higher levels of self-esteem and confidence while validating their efforts to become college learners (Rendon, 1994). Graham and Cockriel (1996) noted in their study that a positive college experience contributed to student development, academic competency, and persistence.

Student Portfolio Assessment. Colleges interested in measuring student academic and noncognitive growth over a stated period of time should consider employing student portfolios. Much can be learned from allowing students and their instructors to collaborate and select a collection of graded student projects and assignments to include in a portfolio covering a substantial period of time. Such projects can often be more reflective of student growth than most one-time "snapshot" standardized assessments. The use of portfolios has become popular with adult students who return to college after varying lengths of time, by those who seek credit for previous work experience, and by students who desire to document their formal classroom- and field-based learning experiences. Barnett (1995) stated that more college faculty members are adopting portfolio assessments as a variable means to assess student performance and are moving away from standardized tests, written papers, and accumulation of class credits as the primary means to measure student learning.

A benefit of student portfolios is that their content can be used as a mechanism for collaboration between faculty members and students. In addition, the coaching and mentoring process makes the portfolio a collaborative and collective activity rather than an independent project (Barnett, 1995). Portfolios may prove to be a comprehensive and effective assessment measure for college faculty and students.

Value-Added Assessments. Assessment that measures student growth over a given period exemplifies a "value-added" approach and provides a more holistic evaluation of student performance and development (Astin, Tsui, and Avalos, 1996). The results of value-added assessments can be used as a feedback mechanism to create environments that will ensure success in college for minority students while helping them to attain their educational goals.

Contemporary educators recognize the value of teaching students how to analyze, reason, evaluate, develop their own opinions, and become dynamic leaders (Rane-Szostak, Robertson, and Fisher, 1996). The need to evaluate overall student outcomes and experiences through value-added assessments can help educators determine educational gains over time while addressing students' perception of their educational experiences. A benefit of value-added assessments is the feedback that is shared among instructors and students after an assessment is undertaken at the beginning, midpoint, and completion of a student's program of study. Such efforts enable students to evaluate their growth over time. Value-added assessments allow students to express what they have learned from attending college, along with other aspects of the college experience that cannot be measured by standardized tests alone.

Community college leaders have noted that for many years traditional measures of institutional quality were not appropriate when applied to community colleges (Heaney, 1990). As an alternative, many community colleges throughout the United States have moved toward value-added approaches to assessment. From an institutional perspective, value-added assessment is not merely measuring how well students perform on assessment measures but also how institutions affect student outcomes. In attempting to employ value-added assessments, community colleges have demonstrated their willingness to assess whether college experiences have benefited students' overall lives.

Although value-added assessments have useful implications for community colleges, they are often criticized for not meeting state requirements for assessing student outcomes (Heaney, 1990). Despite the growing number of states increasing funding for the assessment of performance outcomes, value-added assessments of the overall college experience remain underfunded and ignored. The lack of serious consideration for implementing alternative measures such as value-added assessments makes it difficult for community colleges to move beyond examinations that only attempt to measure academic competency. Today, the importance placed on student achievement as measured by standardized tests appears to outweigh the overall benefits that the college experience may have on students as measured by value-added assessments.

Conclusion

Although average scores for all students continue to increase, multiple studies have revealed that minority students, with the exception of Asian Americans, have performed at levels below those of their white peers. Correlations to students' socioeconomic status, cultural background, and underpreparation were mentioned as the possible reasons for the level of minority student performance on the SAT. Conversely, recent studies challenge the validity of test measures and suggest that standardized achievement testing does not have a reliable predictability value in terms of identifying later success in college. Critics charge that such measures misclassify students who do not possess the typical educational preparation and life experiences of the average middle-class American student.

A rationale for employing alternative assessment does involve overcoming standardized test validity and predictive reliability issues, but more important, it also concerns deriving a more holistic understanding of student outcomes. To provide college educators with supplemental and alternative approaches to standardized testing, several evaluative measures were introduced: student self-assessment, personal and social growth evaluations, portfolios, and value-added assessments. Alternative assessments can be used to complement existing traditional assessment measures. Self-assessment provides students with the opportunity to examine their learning processes and describe their learning experiences, and reflect on the meaning of that learning. Personal and social growth evaluations can be used to gauge the level of student development over a period of time, with an aim to instilling in students a positive self-concept, which has been shown to be associated with higher levels of motivation and academic success. Portfolios can be employed to allow student control of the type of information and materials to be included in the portfolio that is later assessed in conjunction with an instructor to determine student knowledge, skills, and disposition of course instruction. Finally, the value-added approach toward assessing student performance and persistence in college provides a more equitable form of evaluation because it assesses student achievement at the beginning, midpoint, and completion of the undergraduate experience.

The idea of using alternative approaches to assess student learning, performance, and persistence in college is not new. In a political era that ties increased educational funding to improved student performance, discussions surrounding appropriate assessment measures have become highly spirited and contentious. An important challenge for educators remains the selection and administration of comprehensive assessment measures that best capture student performance across cognitive and noncognitive domains and over a defined period of time. Because college educators have been charged with employing assessment strategies that fairly address diverse student learning styles and experiences, the use of alternative assessments can enhance the evaluation process by adding a unique set of measures to more traditional methods.

References

Armstrong, B., Barnes R., and Takabata, G. *Skills Testing and Disproportionate Impact: An Analysis of Reading and Writing Test Performance of Students in the San Diego Community College District.* San Diego, Calif.: San Diego College District Research and Planning, 1991. (ED 346 938)

Astin, A., Tsui, L., and Avalos, J. *Degree Attainment Rates at American Colleges and Universities: Effects of Race, Gender, and Institutional Type.* Los Angeles: Higher Education Research Institution, 1996. (ED 400 749)

Barnett, B. G. "Portfolio Use in Educational Leadership Preparation Programs: From Theory to Practice." *Innovative Higher Education,* 1995, *19,* 197–206.

Carlson, S. "Minority Students Posted Slight Increase in College Enrollment in 1997." *Chronicle of Higher Education,* Dec. 17, 1999, pp. 1–4.

Chenoweth, K. "SAT, ACT Scores Increase." *Black Issues in Higher Education,* 1996, *13,* 6–8.

Chenoweth, K. "A Measurement of What?" *Black Issues in Higher Education,* 1997, *14,* 18–24.

College Board. *College Board Seniors National Report.* New York: The College Board, 1999.

Corwin, M. *And Still We Rise: The Trials and Triumphs of Twelve Gifted Inner-City Children.* New York: Morrow, 2000.

Cress, C. "ERIC Review: Measuring Success Through Assessment and Testing." *Community College Review,* 1996, *24*(1), 39–52.

Gerardi, S. "Academic Self-Concept as a Predictor of Academic Success Among Minority and Low Socioeconomic Status Students." *Journal of College Student Development,* 1990, *31,* 402–407.

Graham, S. W., and Cockriel, I. W. "Indexes to Assess Social and Personal Development and College Impact." *College Student Journal,* 1996, *30,* 502–515.

Heaney, B. "The Assessment of Educational Outcomes." *ERIC Digest,* 1990. (ED 346 082)

House, D. J., and Keeley, E. J. "Predictive Validity of College Admissions Test Scores for American Indian Students." *Journal of Psychology,* 1997, *131,* 572–574.

Jalomo Jr., R. "Institutional Policies That Promote Persistence Among First-Year Community College Students." In B. K. Townsend and S. Twombly (eds.), *Community Colleges: Policy in the Future Context.* Norwood, N.J.: Ablex, 2000.

Kiger, D. M. "Self-Assessing General Education Outcomes at a Community College." *Community College Review,* 1994, *23,* 49–57.

Lederman, D. "Persistent Racial Gap in SAT Scores Fuels Affirmative Action Debate." *Chronicle of Higher Education,* Oct. 30, 1998, pp. 1–5.

Murray, D. "The War Against Testing." *Commentary,* 1998, *106,* 34–37.

Osterlind, S. "A National Review of Scholastic Achievement in General Education." *ASHE-ERIC Higher Education Reports,* 1997, *25,* 1–94.

Owen, D., and Doer, M. *None of the Above: The Truth Behind the SAT.* Lanham, Md.: Rowman & Littlefield, 1999.

Rane-Szostak, D., Robertson, J. F., and Fisher, J. "Issues in Measuring Critical Thinking: Meeting the Challenge." Journal of Nursing Education, *35,* 5–11. New York: McGraw-Hill, 1996.

Rendon, L. I. "Validating Culturally Diverse Students: Toward a New Model of Learning and Student Development." *Innovative Higher Education,* 1994, *19,* 33–51.

Roach, R. "A Test-Taking Frenzy." *Black Issues in Higher Education,* 1999, *16,* 12–13.

Sacks, P. *Standardized Minds.* New York: Perseus Books, 1999.

Terenzini, T. T., and others. "First-Generation College Students: Characteristics, Experiences, and Cognitive Development." *Research in Higher Education,* 1996, *37,* 1–22.

U.S. Department of Education, National Center for Education Statistics. *Digest of Education Statistics.* Washington, D.C.: Office of Educational Research and Improvement, 1998.

ROMERO JALOMO JR. is director of Extended Opportunity Programs and Services at Hartnell College, Salinas, California.

2

This chapter reports findings of a study of students attending selected public two-year colleges. A comparative analysis of white and nonwhite students' perceptions of career and educational goals is presented.

Community College Students' Career and Educational Goals

Frankie Santos Laanan

Community colleges make winners out of ordinary people.
—Leslie Koltai (1993)

Community colleges provide the opportunity for people from all walks of life to advance their education and careers, regardless of their educational background. This democratic environment is appealing to ethnic minority students who seek to improve their lives through education. By providing both an academic and a vocational curriculum, community colleges are the ideal place for individuals to explore their educational and career goals. The purpose of this chapter is twofold: (1) to provide a synthesis of the literature on student attitudes toward career and educational goals, and (2) to present the results of a study that examines the extent to which students' attitudes and perceptions about these life goals differ according to their ethnicity.

Community colleges enroll a substantial percentage of ethnic minorities, women, and nontraditional students. According to the American Association of Community Colleges (Phillippe and Patton, 2000), nationally, about 30 percent of enrollments consist of minority students. Of all enrollees, 58 percent are women, and the enrollment of older students and baccalaureate degree holders who are seeking retraining or new careers is growing. For the majority of individuals, graduating from high school and enrolling immediately in a four-year college or university is considered the traditional route; however, today, attending a community college upon graduating from high school is becoming a popular route, especially among underrepresented groups. Whether because of poverty, lack of academic preparation, or vocational interests (Dougherty, 1994), the option of attending a community college can be viewed as opening college opportunities for many students. In fact, of all first-time students attending higher education institutions each year, almost half attend a community college (Laanan, 2000; Phillippe and Patton, 2000).

Historically, education has been viewed as a springboard to increasing an individual's social status intellectually, professionally, and personally. Today, obtaining an education beyond high school is critical not only for participation in a competitive global market but also as a means of gaining the technical skills and knowledge important to compete in a rapidly changing marketplace (Laanan, 1995). More than ever community colleges are viewed as the segment of America's higher education system that plays a critical role in training the current and future workforce. These institutions are also playing a role in helping to narrow the digital divide (Phillippe and Valiga, 2000) by providing computer skills to a substantial number of students. Research has documented the value of obtaining an education beyond high school. Most of these studies focus on the extent to which there is a positive relationship between education and earnings (Grubb, 1996; Sanchez and Laanan, 1998).

Community colleges successfully serve many individuals' educational and career goals. For many students attending community colleges, the subbaccalaureate credential is the primary educational objective and serves as the impetus for opportunity and social mobility (Grubb, 1996). According to the National Center for Education Statistics (1999), the highest number of certificates awarded in 1996–97 was in the area of health professions (23,401), followed by protective services (10,000), business management and administration services (8,230), transportation and material moving workers (4,278), mechanics and repairers (3,961), and vocational home economics (3,599). The majority of individuals trained in these programs secure positions in the world of work that lead to high-skill, high-wage careers. Other students choose to attend community college for the first two years and then transfer to a four-year institution to attain their baccalaureate degree (Cohen and Brawer, 1996; Laanan, 1998). The highest number of associate's degrees was awarded in liberal/general studies and humanities (167,448), followed by health professions and related sciences (76,848), business management and administration services (71,766), and engineering-related technologies (20,208) (NCES, 1999). Interestingly, a growing number of individuals with baccalaureate degrees are choosing to attend community colleges to obtain specialized skills in computer, health, and other related technologies.

Literature Review

Many students attend community colleges to enhance their work skills and opportunities. Ethnic minority (that is, African American, Asian American, Hispanic/Latino, and Native American) students' different cultural perspectives on work and education may lead to different goals and experiences at the community college.

The Big Picture. In an effort to better understand community college students nationally, the American Association of Community Colleges recently collaborated with the American Council on Education (ACE) to develop a student survey (Phillippe and Valiga, 2000). The *Faces of the Future* survey, which was administered in Fall 1999, collected information from credit and noncredit students from around the nation. Data from over a hundred thousand students at 245 community colleges in forty-one states were collected in various areas, including student demographics, computer skills, student growth in academic and workplace skills, and overall college satisfaction. The following is a summary of findings related to students' educational and career goals:

Among credit students, 60 percent indicated that a major reason for taking classes at the community college was to meet the requirements for their chosen occupation.

Among credit students, 83 percent responded that they were satisfied or very satisfied with their community college.

Eleven percent of credit students and 30 percent of noncredit students reported that they had never used the Internet.

A substantial number of students come to community colleges to obtain computer skills.

Nearly 20 percent of credit and noncredit respondents reported that they learned to use a computer for personal and work-related tasks while in college.

This study reinforces the notion that many students attend community colleges to augment their occupational skills and increase their employability. However, this study does not examine the possible differences between ethnic minority and white students.

Minority Student Experiences. Research has been conducted that examines the attitudes and educational experiences of ethnic minority students. Several of these studies examined students' participation in vocational programs and the factors that influenced their occupational and career choices. Other studies examined students' choice of major and future occupational goals (Boyer, 1993).

To understand the factors that enhance or impede student progress in the successful completion of a technical-occupational program at selected colleges, a two-year study was conducted by El Paso Community College District in Texas (Texas Higher Education Coordinating Board, 1991). Beginning in 1989, the Assessing Minority Opportunities in Vocational Education project collected data from minority students regarding their perceptions of college practices. This two-phase study entailed collecting data from minority and nonminority students in technical-occupational programs. Specifically, the student surveys recorded demographic variables, reasons for entering programs, overall satisfaction, services, and quality of instructors. Based on this study, the report recommended that counseling should orient minority students toward success in their classroom performance and career ambitions. In terms of financial aid, the office should strive for optimal assistance to students and there should be an increase of work-study and job placement programs.

In an effort to erase the negative attitudes toward vocational education among black and Hispanic students in vocational and technical education programs, a model was developed at Dawson Technical Institute in Chicago (Illinois State Board of Education, 1991). This model, which incorporates an interrelated network of various services, helps program staff members recruit, counsel, and, upon completion of vocational programs, assist minority students in finding programs or employment related to their career goals. The model incorporates a team approach that formalizes the processes through which departments in the institution work together to resolve student problems and institutional concerns. The model consists of eight components: (1) recruitment, (2) intake/admissions, (3) assessment, (4) counseling/career planning, (5) financial aid/registration, (6) program placement/retention, (7) job placement, and (8) follow-up/evaluation.

Employing an ethnographic methodology, Hull (1992) conducted a three-year study in which she tracked a group of "at-risk" low-income students enrolled in a community college banking and finance program. At-risk students often rely on public assistance and face challenging life circumstances that may interfere with completing their education. Most of the students in the study were African American women, many of whom were older and returning to school in hopes of improving their skills and getting better jobs. Other participants in the study were younger single mothers who wanted to get off public assistance and find a better way to support their families. Specifically, the research sought to understand the relationship between literacy skills and vocational education and work. Short- and long-term recommendations were advanced. Short-term improvements include matching job placement to students' aspirations, attending to job retention as well as job placement, and integrating literacy instruction into the vocational program. Long-term improvements include investing in long-term employment, creating opportunities for full-time employment, providing child-care services, and creating career paths and making them visible.

A study was conducted to examine the extent of family influence on occupational and career choices (Clayton and others, 1993) between Mexican American and non-Mexican American students. A group of more than two thousand eighth-grade, twelfth-grade, and community college students from eleven Texas school districts and three community colleges, as well as five hundred parents, were surveyed. The researchers compared the responses of students and their parents, and found that, compared with their non-Mexican American counterparts, Mexican American students perceived their parents to have a greater influence on occupational and educational decisions. Furthermore, financing their college education was a major concern among Mexican American parents and students alike.)

In her study of Vietnamese students, Boyer (1993) examined students enrolled in two English-as-a-Second Language (ESL) courses at Golden West College in California. The purpose of the study was to investigate the prospective majors and careers chosen by these students. The study employed a mixed-method approach. Students wrote an essay on their ideal job and completed a questionnaire, which probed the different factors that influenced their career choice (for example, salary, prestige, and nature of work). Finally, students participated in formal and informal interviews and a computer-oriented career exploration experience. Among ESL students, the health care field was the most popular. The most common reasons for their interest in this career path included a desire to help people, followed by high salaries, job security, and interest in science.

(In a recent study sponsored by the Carnegie Foundation, Boyer (1997) examined 1,614 tribal college students' attitudes and outcomes in four areas: student services, instruction, campus climate, and curriculum. The main objective of this study was to provide a comprehensive profile of tribal college students and student opinion. Students at tribal colleges expressed high satisfaction with the staff, instructors, and curriculum. Furthermore, students indicated that job training, affordability, personal interactions with faculty and staff, and support services were important factors in the satisfaction they felt with their college experience.)

The previous studies cited provide useful information about factors that influence students' decisions about or perceptions of education and work. (Particularly for minority students, the literature suggests that family and academic support factors play an important role not only in learning about the possible career choices but also in facilitating or enhancing academic success. Strategies such as job placement programs and addressing individuals' aspirations promote success beyond graduation (Hull, 1992; Illinois State Board of Education, 1991). Boyer (1993) found that Vietnamese students' career aspirations were motivated not only by the desire for individual advancement but also by the desire to provide service to the community. Family and community influences may be greater for ethnic minority students from collectivist cultures.

However, most of these studies are based on data from a single institution, and thus provide only a snapshot of what is going on in a particular educational environment. A study that has a larger sample size, which collects various information about students' background and career and educational goals, will provide researchers and policymakers with a better understanding not only of their affective attitudes but also of the patterns that may be evident. The research conducted by AACC and ACE attempts to paint a clearer picture of students, both credit and noncredit, enrolled in the nation's community colleges and the impact that these institutions have on these students. However, their analysis does not investigate any differences between ethnic minority and white students.

Objectives of the Study

The purpose of this study is to investigate the extent to which two groups of students at community colleges differ with respect to their background characteristics, attitudes, and perceptions about career and educational goals. The sample for this cross-sectional study is the cohort of first-time full-time freshmen enrolled in public two-year colleges in Fall 1996, who responded to the freshman survey conducted by the Cooperative Institutional Research Program, which is sponsored by the American Council on Education and the Higher Education Research Institute at the University of California, Los Angeles. Students completed the Student Information Form (SIF) at the beginning of the Fall 1996 term, and during registration, freshmen orientation, and the first few weeks of classes. The SIF, which contains over 250 items, collects information that includes biographic and demographic data, high school experiences, career plans, educational aspirations, current attitudes, and other affective measures.

Included in the sample are two-year colleges offering associate's degrees as well as vocational certificates. The sample for this study includes 10,638 first-time full-time freshmen attending fifty-one public community colleges across the United States. Based on the American Council on Education (ACE) coding scheme, the following is a breakdown of representation by region: East (42.5 percent), Midwest (16.3 percent), South (20.0 percent), and West (21.2 percent). The study includes students from two groups: nonwhite (2,639) and white (7,999). The nonwhite group consists of the following racial/ethnic groups: American Indian, Asian, black, and Chicano/ Latino. The Chicano/Latino category includes Mexican American/Chicano, Puerto Rican, and Other Latino. In terms of students' racial/ethnic background, they are as follows: white (73.5 percent), black (9.8 percent), American Indian (2.3 percent), Asian (2.5 percent), Chicano/Latino (9.6 percent), Other (2.3 percent). The rationale for collapsing the nonwhite racial groups into one category was to achieve a group sufficiently large for statistical comparisons. Although the focus of this study is to examine two groups of students (nonwhite and white) in an effort to understand patterns, combining the nonwhite group may conceal within-group differences.

Frequencies and cross-tabulations were used to examine the relationship between selected items and the two primary student groups (nonwhite and white). In addition, a t-test of independent samples was performed to compare the means of one variable for the two student groups. The t-test was used to test the null hypothesis that the means of the groups are the same. For this study, statistical significance was determined by probability values of less than .001.

Results

Table 2.1 illustrates a cross-tabulation analysis of the background characteristics of nonwhite and white students. Overall, half of the students are women. Slightly less than half (45.3 percent) of the nonwhite students are eighteen or younger, compared with 57 percent of white students. A little less than half of the nonwhite and one-third of the white students are between the ages of nineteen and twenty-four. In terms of miles from permanent home to the college, more than half of the nonwhite students lived ten miles or less from the college, compared with 34.8 percent of the white students. About two-thirds of the students from both groups indicated that they planned to live with their parents during the fall. Approximately two-thirds of both groups indicated that this institution was their first choice (60.1 percent for nonwhite students versus 68.8 percent for white students).

In comparing the educational background of students' parents, close to two-thirds of the nonwhite students had parents whose schooling had not gone beyond high school, compared with about half of the white

Table 2.1 Background Characteristics by Student Racial Group Status (n = 10,638)

	Percentage Among	
	Nonwhite[1] (n = 2,639)	White (n = 7,999)
Gender		
Female	56.6	51.7
Age		
18 or younger	45.3	57.0
19–24	47.1	38.4
25 or over	7.6	4.6
Miles from home to college		
10 or less	59.1	34.8
11–50	33.6	45.2
51–100	5.4	8.6
101 or more	9.5	11.4
Plan to live during fall		
With parents	67.8	64.5
In private home	17.2	15.2
In dormitory	8.6	16.5
Other	6.4	3.8
Choice of this institution		
First choice	60.1	68.8
Second choice	22.1	19.5
Third choice	9.6	6.0

(continued)

Table 2.1 Background Characteristics by Student Racial Group Status (n = 10,638)

	Percentage Among	
	Nonwhite[1] (n = 2,639)	White (n = 7,999)
Father's education		
Some high school or less	35.8	12.6
High school graduate	28.0	36.9
Some college	18.0	21.2
College graduate or higher	18.2	29.3
Mother's education		
Some high school or less	33.6	10.1
High school graduate	28.4	39.3
Some college	19.2	23.5
College graduate or higher	18.9	27.1
Parental annual income		
$24,999 or below	55.8	20.9
$25,000–49,999	26.5	34.1
$50,000–74,999	10.9	28.0
$75,000+	6.9	17.2
Highest degree aspiration at this institution		
None	4.8	7.1
Vocational certificate	5.3	3.7
Associate's	69.6	72.4
Other	3.0	2.5
Highest degree aspiration planned		
None	7.1	4.0
Vocational certificate	3.0	2.3
Associate's	11.3	12.4
Bachelor's	28.4	35.0
Master's	33.9	33.8
Doctorate	16.2	12.6

Note: The nonwhite category includes the following racial/ethnic groups: American Indian, Asian, Black, and Chicano-Latino.

Source: Cooperative Institutional Research Program, UCLA Higher Education Research Institute.

students' parents. This finding suggests two things: (1) nonwhite students were likely to be first-generation students, and (2) white students were more likely to have parents with higher educational attainment levels. In terms of students' reported parental annual income, more than half of the nonwhite students reported their parental income to be $24,999 or below, compared with one-fifth of the white students' parents. In general, white students were more likely to have parents with higher annual income ($50,000 or more).

Two questions on the survey probed students' educational aspirations. The first question asked students to indicate their highest degree aspiration at their present institution. Nonwhite and white students responded similarly to this question; that is, they indicated the associate's degree as their highest degree aspiration at this institution (69.6 percent of the nonwhite students versus 72.4 percent of the white students). A second question asked students to indicate their highest degree planned overall. Interestingly, the two groups also responded similarly to this question. About one-fourth of nonwhite and one-third of white students indicated that they aspired to the bachelor's degree; another third for both groups indicated the master's degree. Some students indicated the doctorate as their highest degree planned overall (16.2 percent of the nonwhite students versus 12.6 percent of the white students). Although Table 2.1 illustrates descriptive information about students' highest degree aspirations (that is, at this [two-year] institution, and planned overall), the findings suggest that both nonwhite and white students planned to transfer to a four-year institution to complete the bachelor's degree. Furthermore, a third of both groups indicated that the master's degree was their highest degree planned overall. In general, these findings suggest that although students chose to begin their postsecondary education at a two-year college, a substantial percentage of them have aspirations beyond the associate's degree.

One of the goals of this study is to examine factors that have influenced nonwhite and white students' decision to go to college. On the survey, students were asked to respond to the question, "In deciding to go to college, how important to you was each of the following reasons?" on a three-point scale from 1 = *not important*, 2 = *somewhat important*, to 3 = *very important*. Figure 2.1 displays a bar chart comparing nonwhite and white students on eight items. The figure reports only the percentage of students responding "very important" on each of the items. The highest response for both groups was on the item "get a better job." That is, 82.7 percent of nonwhite and 80 percent of white students indicated this reason for deciding to go to college. The second-highest response was "make more money," followed by "learn more things." Nonwhite students had substantially higher responses on the following items: parents' wish (parents wanted me to go) (52.3 percent versus 38.4 percent), improve study skills (66.8 percent versus 37.3 percent), gain general education (70.3 percent versus 53.8 percent), and become more cultured (43.5 percent versus 26.9 percent), compared with their white counterparts. For both groups, the lowest response was on the item "couldn't find a job" (18.4 percent versus 9 percent). The results from the t-test revealed statistically significant differences on six of the eight items. Nonwhite students were more likely to indicate that internal and external factors—such as parental influence, their inability to find a job, and their desire to gain a general education, improve reading and study skills, become more cultured, and learn things that

Figure 2.1 Reasons for Attending College, Percentage Responding "Very Important"

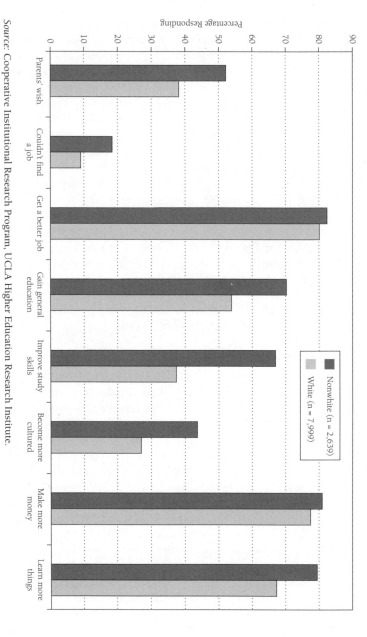

Source: Cooperative Institutional Research Program, UCLA Higher Education Research Institute.

interested them—were important reasons for attending college, compared with the responses of white students. The two items that did not yield statistically significant differences included "get a better job" and "make more money," to which nonwhite and white students responded similarly. These two items were the most important reasons for attending college for all the students.

Figure 2.2 shows the comparative findings of students' responses to reasons that influenced their decision to attend the college they were attending in 1996. Students responded to each item on a three-point scale from 1 = *not important*, 2 = *somewhat important*, to 3 = *very important*. The bar chart reports students responding "very important" to each item. On the survey, the question read, "How important was each reason in your decision to come to this particular college?" Slightly less than half indicated that the college's low tuition was a very important reason for choosing this college. Furthermore, over one-third of the students reported that the good academic reputation, opportunity to live near home, and the rate at which graduates get good jobs were very important reasons for attending this community college. Relatively few students indicated that relatives' wishes and the advice of teachers were very important reasons for attending this college. Finally, nonwhite students had higher responses on these items: "offered financial aid" (35.6 percent of nonwhite students versus 23.1 percent of white students) and "offers special programs" (30.7 percent of nonwhite students versus 15.6 percent of white students). On the other hand, white students had higher responses on these items: "low tuition" (49 percent of white students versus 44.7 percent of nonwhite students), "live near home" (33.2 percent of white students versus 30.8 percent of nonwhite students), and "size of college" (24.3 percent of white students versus 19 percent of nonwhite students).

The results from the t-test revealed statistically significant differences on all but one of the items. White students were more likely to indicate that factors such as low tuition, living near home, and attending a school about the size of this college were important reasons for attending college. Conversely, nonwhite students were more likely to indicate that relatives' wishes, the advice of teachers, financial aid, educational programs, and the reputation that this college's graduates get good jobs were important reasons for choosing this college, compared with the responses of white students. The one item that did not yield a statistically significant difference was "This college has a very good academic reputation." In other words, both nonwhite and white students were similar in their perceptions about the academic reputation of the two-year college.

The research literature provides evidence that students choose to attend a community college for various reasons. Furthermore, the trend of minority students enrolled in community colleges continues to show the important role these institutions play in providing educational access and opportunity for a diverse clientele.

Figure 2.2 Community College Students' Reasons for Choosing This College, Percentage Responding "Very Important"

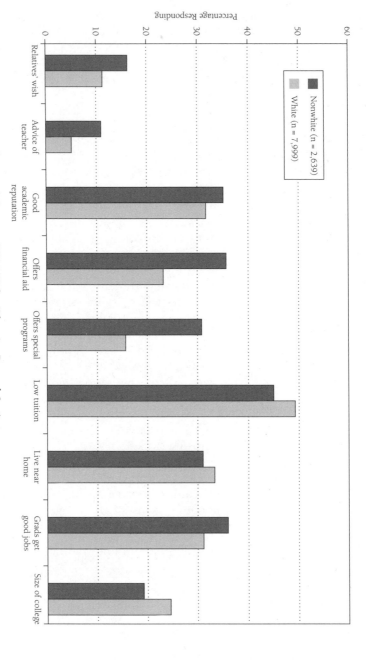

Source: Cooperative Institutional Research Program, UCLA Higher Education Research Institute.

Discussion and Conclusion

The purpose of this study was to examine two groups of students and the extent to which they differed in terms of their background characteristics, attitudes, and educational and career goals when enrolling for the first time in institutions of higher education. Although this was a descriptive study, the findings provide several insights into our understanding of traditional-age white and nonwhite students attending selected public community colleges. The popular option of attending a community college is supported by the finding that over half of the nonwhite and white students indicated that the community college was their first choice to begin their postsecondary education.

Interestingly, a little less than three-fourths of the students indicated that the associate's degree was their highest degree planned at the community college. When asked about their highest degree aspiration overall, slightly more than 10 percent indicated the associate's degree. Among nonwhite and white students, aspiring toward the bachelor's degree and the master's degree was common. This finding suggests that these students are choosing to attend the community college to complete their first two years of education with the intention of transferring to a four-year institution. Because this study does not allow for follow-up, it is not possible to measure the extent to which these students change their educational objective or ultimately transfer to a senior institution. A longitudinal design would be needed in order to fully understand the changes either from the student development or the aspiration perspectives.

The results of this study provide evidence that both nonwhite and white students choose the community college because of low tuition costs, in addition to having the desire to live near home. About one-third of students also indicated that graduates' job placement rates and the college's good academic reputation were important reasons for choosing this college. This is a positive finding because among many high school students the community college is often thought of as an extension of high school. This notion continues to be perpetuated because of its open-access admissions standards.

The results of this study provide evidence that traditional-age nonwhite and white students possess positive perceptions of community colleges. A majority of the students indicated that attending the community college was their first choice to begin their postsecondary education. In terms of their reasons for attending college, getting a better job, making more money, and learning more things were very important among both nonwhite and white students. This finding supports the notion that students' perceptions about obtaining an education beyond a high school diploma will facilitate these opportunities. This finding is consistent with the research that suggests that there is a positive relationship between educational attainment and earnings.

The findings that emerged with regard to students' reasons for attending college raise interesting points. First, the statistically significant differences favored nonwhite students; that is, nonwhite students scored higher on all but two of the items. This suggests that nonwhite students perceive internal and external factors as more important, compared with the perceptions of their white counterparts. However, it is important that these findings not be misinterpreted. Although the differences are statistically significant, the question that needs to be raised is to what extent these differences are practical. Second, the two groups seem to be more similar than they are different in terms of what they indicated as being "very important" reasons for attending college. Finally, the practical significance of these findings is that both groups indicate personal, educational, and external factors as being important in their decision to attend community college.

Interestingly, regarding students' reasons for choosing this college, two items that are especially worth mentioning are "low tuition" and "grads get good jobs." Specifically, white students were more likely to indicate that the low tuition was an important factor in choosing the community college, compared with the general response of their nonwhite counterparts, who were more likely to indicate that information about the college's graduates getting good jobs was an important factor in their choosing this college.

The literature suggests that for minority students various external factors play a role in influencing educational objectives as well as career choices. It is clear that students today are becoming "smart consumers," in that they are aware of the demands of a changing marketplace—both locally and globally—and of the requirement to be an active participant. The role of community colleges becomes even more important as they provide a diverse constituency with education and training to meet the demands of the workplace.

Although the focus of the descriptive analysis is on two groups of students (nonwhite and white), it is important to raise the question of "within group" differences. This is particularly important among those in the nonwhite group. Inasmuch as this group includes African American, Asian, American Indian, and Chicano/Latino students, it is plausible that differences in students' perceptions and attitudes will exist. Such perceptual differences would be based on differences in culture and socialization. Further investigation is needed to test this notion. Following this same logic, further analysis by gender might reveal different results for men and women.

In conclusion, the results of this study support the view that attending community college is a worthwhile option among traditional-age students. The importance of securing a better position in the world of work and earning a good living are reasons for young adults to be attending postsecondary institutions. The fact that these young adults hold these beliefs and values and still choose to attend community college suggests that these institutions can give students the springboard they need to achieve their personal and professional goals, allowing them to complete a certificate program or an associate's degree, or to eventually transfer to a four-year institution.

References

Boyer, N. *Vietnamese Choice of Majors at Golden West College.* Huntington Beach, Calif.: Golden West College, 1993. (ED 365 385)

Boyer, P. "First Survey of Tribal College Students Reveals Attitudes." *Tribal College,* 1997, *9*(2), 36–41.

Clayton, K. K., and others. *Family Influence Over the Occupational and Educational Choices of Mexican American Students.* Berkeley, Calif.: National Center for Research in Vocational Education, 1993. (ED 367 786)

Cohen, A. M., and Brawer, F. B. *The American Community College.* (3rd ed.) San Francisco: Jossey-Bass, 1996.

Dougherty, K. J. *The Contradictory College: The Conflicting Origins, Impacts, and Futures of the Community College.* Albany, N.Y.: State University of New York Press, 1994.

Grubb, W. N. *Working in the Middle: Strengthening Education and Training for the Mid-Skilled Labor Force.* San Francisco: Jossey-Bass, 1996.

Hull, G. *Their Chances? Slim and None. An Ethnographic Account of the Experiences of Low-Income People of Color in a Vocational Program and at Work.* Berkeley, Calif.: National Center for Research in Vocational Education, 1992. (ED 351 553)

Illinois State Board of Education. *A Model to Improve the Quality and Quantity of Minority Student Participation in Vocational-Technical Education Programs.* Springfield, Ill.: Department of Adult, Vocational and Technical Education, 1991. (ED 345 011)

Koltai, L. "Community Colleges: Making Winners Out of Ordinary People." In A. Levine (ed.), *Higher Learning in America 1980–2000.* Baltimore, Md.: Johns Hopkins University Press, 1993, pp. 100–113.

Laanan, F. S. *Community Colleges as Facilitators of School-to-Work.* Los Angeles: ERIC Clearinghouse for Community Colleges, 1995. (ED 383 360)

Laanan, F. S. "Beyond Transfer Shock: A Study of Students' College Experiences and Adjustment Process at UCLA." Unpublished doctoral dissertation, School of Education, University of California, Los Angeles, 1998.

Laanan, F. S. "Two-Year College Students' Degree Aspirations." Paper presented at the Association for Institutional Research Annual Forum, Cincinnati, Ohio, May 23, 2000.

National Center for Education Statistics. *Integrated Postsecondary Education Data System (IPEDS) Completions Survey.* Washington, D.C.: U.S. Department of Education, 1999.

Phillippe, K. A., and Patton, M. *National Profile of Community Colleges: Trends and Statistics.* (3rd ed.) Washington, D.C.: American Association of Community Colleges, 2000.

Phillippe, K. A., and Valiga, M. J. *Faces of the Future. A Portrait of America's Community College Student.* Washington, D.C.: American Association of Community Colleges, 2000.

Sanchez, J. R., and Laanan, F. S. (eds.). *Determining the Economic Benefits of Attending Community College.* New Directions for Community Colleges, no. 104. San Francisco: Jossey-Bass, 1998.

Texas Higher Education Coordinating Board. *Assessing Minority Opportunities in Vocational Education (MOVED): A Research Report.* Austin, Tex.: Texas Higher Education Coordinating Board, 1991. (ED 341 447)

FRANKIE SANTOS LAANAN is assistant professor of community college leadership at the University of Illinois at Urbana-Champaign.

3

Successful learning experiences contribute to student motivation and retention and require that educators design programs around learning preferences. This chapter discusses the relationship of learning preferences to motivation and retention and presents a profile of learning preferences of Hispanic and Native American learners.

Motivating and Maximizing Learning in Minority Classrooms

Irene M. Sanchez

At all levels of education, teachers face the challenge of motivating learners and maximizing learning in the classroom. This chapter discusses the influence of teachers' expectations and students' learning styles on the learning environment for minority students. In particular, research on the learning styles of Hispanic and Native American learners at two colleges in the Southwest will be presented, and suggestions for restructuring educational experiences for students in these groups will be provided.

The number of minority students in the country is growing, but their rate of educational attainment is not keeping pace with this growth. The number and proportion of minority students in colleges is increasing. Data from the *Chronicle of Higher Education* (2000) show that from 1976 to 1996 the number of Native American, African American, Asian American, and Hispanic students attending two- and four-year institutions increased from 1.6 to 3.6 million. This represents an increase of 125 percent in twenty years. The proportion of minority students in higher education is also increasing. Between 1976 and 1996, the percentage of enrolled college students who were minorities increased by 63 percent. Although these data indicate gains in access, retention of minority students in higher education has not improved. Table 3.1 illustrates the fact that, with the exception of Asians, minority groups lag behind in educational attainment.

Institutions are seeking new strategies to address this gap between access and educational attainment by examining classroom dynamics. The work of Vincent Tinto (1987, 1997, 1999) creates a bridge between motivation and learning styles and student persistence research. This "bridge" may provide educators with ideas for successful strategies that enhance

Table 3.1 Level of College Attainment of U.S. Population by Racial and Ethnic Group: 1900

Racial or Ethnic Group	Number of Adults in Millions	Percentage with Associate's Degree	Percentage with Bachelor's Degree	Percentage with Graduate or Professional Degree
Native Americans	1.1	6.4	6.1	3.3
Blacks	16.8	5.3	7.5	3.8
Asians	4.3	7.7	22.7	13.9
Hispanics	11.2	4.8	5.9	3.3
Whites	132.0	6.3	13.9	7.7

Source: U.S. Department of Education, National Center for Education Statistics, as reported in *Chronicle of Higher Education Almanac, 1998–99,* 2000.

opportunities for higher educational attainment for minority students. Tinto (1997) emphasizes the importance of the classroom experience in student persistence. He argues that the "classroom may be the only place where students and faculty meet" and that the classroom is the "crossroads where social and academic integration occurs" (p. 599). He explains how social and academic integration enhances learning opportunities, which may lead to persistence by providing students with supportive experiences that meet both academic and social needs. It may be that the lack of cultural appropriateness in some college classroom environments makes it impossible for minority students to feel "socially integrated" with what is happening in the classroom.

Effects of Teacher Expectations on Student Achievement

A brief review of motivation research may shed some light on factors that have an impact on academic achievement and student persistence. Brophy (1986) discusses the effect of teacher expectations and teacher behavior on students and posits that the teacher's beliefs about the abilities of students, as well as the students' perceptions about their own abilities, affect the opportunities afforded them. Lower expectations result in limited opportunities for some students. Thus, student motivation and the effort students devote to academic tasks can be circumscribed by teacher expectations. Students recognize the lower expectation level and, over time, their self-concept and motivation may decline until the potential to achieve is diminished. This may lead to limited educational success, which in turn affects the desire to remain in school.

Expanding upon this discussion, Bamburg (1994) identifies several factors that contribute to lower teacher expectations, including misuses of testing and misdiagnoses of students' potential to learn. Based upon "expectancy times value" theory, he reinforces the assumption that students will not invest effort into even highly valued tasks if they believe that they are not capable of achieving the task with reasonable effort. This body of research indicates that expectations for minority student academic achievement may be tainted by lack of information or by misconceived notions of lower abilities.

These notions are often based upon lower scores on standardized tests and what Bamburg (1994) calls "educational predestination" and misdiagnosing of learning potential, particularly in urban schools, which consist primarily of minority students. The report produced by the U.S. Department of Education's Task Force on Hispanic Dropouts (1998) describes the "academic triage" that occurs in schools with limited resources. These schools frequently channel resources away from programs for minority students, based upon the perception that they have less potential for learning. Thus, minority students are routinely "sacrificed" and afforded fewer opportunities to learn challenging subject matter.

Learning Styles Research

In addition to efficacy perceptions, success in learning is influenced by the student's learning preferences and learning style. An examination of this research may also provide some useful insights into successful strategies to use with minority students.

The assessment of learning styles and the impact of matching learning with teaching style has been the focus of many studies. Dunn, Dunn, and Price (1981) report that learning style research has provided useful information about the "effects of environmental, sociological and cognitive preferences on the achievement of students" (p. 50). Guild (1994) points out that educators must consider the connection between culture and learning style, and that effective educational practices derive from an understanding of the way individuals learn and the impact of culture upon learning preferences.

Anderson (1988) suggests that culture has considerable influence upon the worldview of individuals, which greatly influences the development of learning preferences. Dunn and Griggs (1995) observe that specific cultural groups tend to have learning style elements that distinguish them from other cultural groups. For example, a culture that values cooperation and places more emphasis upon the good of the group rather than the individual may produce students who have a natural preference for learning environments that allow for cooperation rather than competition.

Aragon (1996) argues that a student's culture provides the conceptual knowledge for a set of tools that he or she brings to the learning environment. Based on Euro-American cultural concepts, the American educational system does not allow opportunities for minority students to employ their culturally specific tools, because learning involves application of one's own framework (Aragon, 1996; Brown, Collins, and Duglid, 1989; Tierney, 1994;

Laden, 1998). Trueba (1991) expands upon the importance of cultural knowledge that is transferred from one generation to another as a factor for the development of higher psychological functions that are necessary for academic achievement. Rendon (1994) concludes that educational systems that are not set up to accommodate minority students create an "invalidating environment" for students who do not fit a particular mold. Aragon (1996) also points out that minority students are often branded as deficient when the prevailing Euro-American yardstick measures them.

Perhaps the influence of culture can be further understood by looking at Jonassen and Grabowski's aptitude-by-interaction (ATI) model (1993), which suggests that learners perceive instruction through their own particular set of "individual difference filters," which may enhance or may prevent learning. ATI provides a relational basis for understanding how a learner's unique components and the demands of the learning task interact to contribute to various learning outcomes. Figure 3.1 illustrates this interaction.

The underlying premise of this relationship is the assumption that learners enter the learning relationship with unique tools or capabilities for learning, certain personality traits, and prior knowledge. Interaction

Figure 3.1 The Relationship of Unique Learner Components and Demands of the Learning Task to Learning Outcomes

Learner's Cognitive Tools
Composed of culturally influenced
cognitive controls and cognitive styles

plus

Learner's Personality Traits
Composed of emotional stability and motivation

plus

Learner's Prior Learning Experiences and Prior Knowledge
Influenced by culture and learning style
and teacher expectations and teacher behavior

plus

Interaction with the Demands of the Learning Task
Influenced by the learning environment
created by teacher expectations and teacher behavior

yield

Positive or Negative Learning Outcomes
Influenced by student expectations, motivation, and effort

with the requirements of the learning task will determine the quality and types of learning outcomes that result.

Learning style research at all grade levels suggests that culture influences the learning process and outcomes, students' preferences affect achievement, and students process information in different ways. It also posits that when teaching strategies match learning styles, positive learning outcomes result (Jonassen and Grabowski, 1993; Guild, 1994; Dunn and Griggs, 1995; Aragon, 1996; and Anderson, 1988).

Most educators would probably agree that the learning styles of white students are most closely aligned with the instructional strategies used at most college campuses across the nation, and that the learning preferences of minority students have been ignored until recently. This lack of information may be an important factor in minority student motivation and retention.

Hispanic and Native American Learners in a College Setting

In order to test the impact of culture on learning preferences, Sanchez (1996) and Aragon (1996) studied the learning style preferences of two groups of Hispanic and Native American learners at colleges in the Southwest. The concurrent studies compared the learning preferences of 240 Hispanics and 206 Native Americans, respectively, with the norms for white students. Both studies used Curry's Theoretical Model of Learning Style Components and Effects (1991). The model analyzes learning preferences at three levels which, when combined, define a learning style.

The motivational maintenance level measures the learner's preferred method for interacting with the environment, including interaction with teachers, peers, and the learning task, persistence and willingness to work at a task, and the level of need that the student brings to the learning situation.

The task engagement level is the interaction between the motivational condition of the learner and the active processing work required by the learning task, and includes attention, participation, methods of study, fact retention and recall, and degree of concentration exhibited by the learner in the new learning situation.

The cognitive strategies level involves the cognitive information processing habits or control systems that the learner brings to the learning situation, including methods of receiving and recording information, based on personal and cultural characteristics.

The model uses three instruments to assess each level. Level one is measured by Friedman and Stritter's Instructional Preference Questionnaire (1976), Grasha and Riechmann's Student Learning Styles Scales (1975), and Rezler and Rezmovic's Learning Preference Inventory (1981). Level two is measured by using Kagan's Matching Familiar Figures Test (1964),

Schmeck, Ribich, and Ramanaiah's Inventory of Learning Processes (1977), and Weinstein's Learning and Studies Strategies Inventory (1987). Finally, Kolb's Learning Styles Inventory (1977), the Myers-Briggs Type Indicator (Myers, 1962), and Witkin, Oltman, Reskin, and Karp's Embedded Figures Test (1971) measure level three.

Data were analyzed by using measures of central tendency, t-tests, chi-square, and factor analysis. The results of the data were used in developing a profile of learning preferences for each of the scales measured by the nine instruments. Demographic factors such as ethnicity, gender, degree of bilingualism, educational level, and age were examined to assess their impact on the scales.

Table 3.2 profiles the learning style preferences that emerged for the study population. The preferences are the scales by which differences in the responses of minority and white students are statistically significant and can be interpreted as strong preferences for the variable or as a strong propensity to use the component as a learning strategy.

Implications for the Design and Delivery of Educational Programs for Hispanic and Native American Students

Awareness and analysis of these significant preferences may be useful in designing instructional programs for these students. At the motivational level, both Hispanic and Native American students exhibited definite preferences for feedback, participation, collaboration, and concrete experiences, in comparison with white students. Classroom environments that create a climate for academic success for these students should take these preferences into consideration. Group work that requires the practical application of abstract theory and emphasizes that what is being learned in the classroom can be applied to real-life experiences would be appropriate. Many students must work while in school, and allowing them to design group projects that apply classroom theories to their work situations would be effective. Group assignments give students the opportunity to plan, carry out, and evaluate activities and to receive feedback from the instructor and peers in a supportive environment. They also allow the teacher to reinforce the positive aspects of the work accomplished by the group. This would also accommodate the Native American preference for teacher-directed activities, as the teacher would provide guidance at appropriate intervals.

At the task engagement level, both groups demonstrated a high propensity for fact retention, elaborative processing, attitude, and reflectivity. A propensity for fact retention and elaborative processing implies an ability to engage in higher-order cognitive processing. In order to support these processes, instructors should design activities that engage the learner in processing and synthesizing different types of information, and making judgments based upon that information. These four factors, when applied to a

Table 3.2 Learning Preferences of Hispanic and Native American Learners

	Motivational Level	Task Engagement Level	Cognitive Strategies Level
Hispanics	*Feedback*: the degree to which students find evaluative mechanisms helpful *Participation over Avoidance*: the desire to participate in classroom activities *Collaborative over Competitive*: Preference to share ideas and work in groups over a desire to perform better than others and compete for grades *Concrete over Abstract*: Preference for tangible, specific, practical tasks over theories, hypotheses, and general principles	*Fact Retention*: Propensity to retain detailed, factual information *Elaborative Processing*: Strategies used to encode new information, such as relating to old information, use of visual imagery, and practical application *Attitude*: Level of interest in learning *Reflective*: Cognitive tempo that involves thinking before acting	*Active Experimentation* Action-based approach to learning *Judgment over Perception*: Preference for using a judgmental (thinking or feeling) rather than a perceptive (sensing or intuitive) process
Native Americans	*Dependent*: Preference for teacher-directed structure and support *Feedback* *Collaborative over Competitive* *Concrete over Abstract*	*Fact Retention* *Elaborative Processing* *Attitude* *Reflective*	*Concrete Experience and Abstract Conceptualization* were equally preferred *Sensing and Thinking* were equally preferred

classroom environment, suggest the need to engage minority students in activities that allow them to examine new information and subject matter (facts to be retained), make sense of it, and verify its validity and relationship to their personal experiences and prior knowledge. Again, group work lends itself to accommodating these factors and also encourages the groups' tendency to be reflective. Within a small group, students can reflect and think before they express their ideas, thus helping them to practice an important skill in an environment that may be more comfortable than a large classroom. Whether group work is used or not, the groups' reflective thinking should be considered by the teacher. Being reflective means that students from these two groups may not be vocal in the classroom, or they may not respond immediately when questioned. The teacher should not interpret this as a sign of lack of interest or knowledge, but should recognize that thinking before speaking is a "cultural tool" that requires processing time. This may require the rethinking of giving participation points that are based solely upon verbal response and discussion in the classroom.

At the cognitive strategy level, the groups differed (Hispanic students showed a preference for active experimentation and judgment over perception) and Native American students showed an equal preference for concrete experiences and abstract conceptualization and thinking.

Activities that would accommodate these preferences require a variety of teaching strategies that focus on the concrete application of abstract concepts with some measure of hands-on experimentation and application of information. The instructor should use a variety of alternative strategies that reach the same teaching objective and give students the option of selecting those activities that best meet their preferred learning style and make the most cultural sense to them. These strategies may include lectures, role-plays, discussion, problem-based scenarios, reactor panels, and job-related projects.

It is important to keep in mind that not all Hispanic and Native American students can be stereotyped as having these learning preferences, as these components were affected by ethnicity, gender, age, and degree of bilingualism. However, they may be useful as a guide in designing instructional strategies for these groups.

Effect on Retention

The elements of the learning community, namely, "shared knowing" and "shared knowledge," that Tinto (1997) proposes appear to fit very closely with the elements that create an inclusive learning environment that may be a good fit with the learning preferences of minority students. As seen in the profiles of Hispanic and Native American learners, both groups have high preferences for participation in active, concrete learning experiences and would probably thrive in an environment where knowledge is applied to real-life situations. They also prefer cooperative situations in which peers help one another learn and can use their culturally learned and respected "tool" of ensuring group over individual success. Both groups also displayed a high propensity for elaborative processing. Participation in linked courses or freshman interest groups would allow them to use this skill in making connections between new and prior knowledge and from one course to another. Seminar-type learning that focuses on problem solving would also allow for opportunities to express ideas in a supportive environment.

Conclusion

The number of minority students is increasing across campuses in America; however, their level of educational attainment is lagging behind that of white students. Minority students are coming to colleges but are not completing degree programs at rates that give them broad access to higher-paying employment and economic status. Instructors who structure their classrooms to consider minority students' "cultural tools" (preferred learning strategies and styles) will allow them to become socially and academically integrated and enable them to make sense of what is happening in the classroom in terms of their own culture and real-life situations.

As college classrooms become more diverse, the challenge for teachers at two- and four-year institutions is to recognize and affirm the cultural diversity of their students and to design environments within the classroom that provide the opportunity for them to excel in the ways in which they prefer to learn. Providing a variety of instructional activities through the use of a wide array of instructional technologies will create environments that encourage active participation, deeper learning, and higher retention for minority students.

References

Anderson, J. A. "Cognitive Styles and Multicultural Populations." *Journal of Teacher Education,* 1988, *39,* 2–9.

Aragon, S. R. "The Development of a Conceptual Framework of Learning for Native American Adult Learners in a Formal Educational Environment." Unpublished doctoral dissertation, Department of Education, University of New Mexico, 1996.

Bamburg, J. D. *Raising Expectations to Improve Student Learning.* Urban Monograph Series. Oakbrook, Ill.: North Central Regional Educational Laboratory, 1994. (ED 378 290)

Brophy, J. *On Motivating Students.* East Lansing, Mich.: Institute for Research on Teaching, Oct. 1986. (ED 276 724)

Brown, J. S., Collins, A., and Duglid, P. "Situated Cognition and the Culture of Learning." *Educational Researcher,* 1989, *18,* 32–42.

Chronicle of Higher Education Almanac, 1998–99, Mar. 2000.

Curry, L. "Patterns of Learning Styles Across Medical Specialties." *Educational Psychology,* 1991, *11*(3–4), 247–277.

Dunn, R., Dunn, K., and Price, C. E. *Productivity, Environmental Survey.* Lawrence, Kans.: Price Systems. 1981.

Dunn, R., and Griggs, S. A. *Multiculturalism and Learning Style: Teaching and Counseling Adolescents.* New York: Praeger, 1995.

Friedman, C. P., and Stritter, F. T. "An Empirical Inventory Comparing Instructional Preferences of Medical and Other Professional Students." *Research in Medical Education Proceedings,* 15th Annual Conference, San Francisco, 1976, pp. 63–68.

Grasha, A. F., and Reichman, S. W. *Student Learning Styles Questionnaire.* Cincinnati, Ohio: University of Cincinnati Faculty Resource Center, 1975.

Guild, P. "The Culture/Learning Style Connection." *Educational Leadership,* 1994, *51*(8), 16–21.

Jonassen, D. H., and Grabowski, B. L., *Handbook of Individual Differences, Learning and Instruction.* Hillsdale, N.J.: Erlbaum, 1993.

Kagan, J. *Matching Familiar Figures Test.* Cambridge, Mass.: Harvard University Press, 1964.

Kolb, D. A. *Learning Styles Inventory: A Self-Description of Preferred Learning Mode.* Boston: McBer, 1977.

Laden, B. T. "An Organizational Response to Welcoming Students of Color." In J. S. Levin (ed.), *Organizational Change in the Community College: A Ripple or a Sea Change?* New Directions for Community Colleges, no. 102. San Francisco: Jossey-Bass, 1998.

Myers, I. B. *The Myers-Briggs Type Indicator.* Palo Alto, Calif.: Consulting Psychologists Press, 1962.

Reichmann, S. W., and Grasha, A. F. "A Rational Approach to Developing and Assessing the Construct Validity of a Student Learning Styles Scale Instrument." *Journal of Psychology,* 1974, *87,* 213–223.

Rendon, L. I. "A Systematic View of Minority Students in Educational Institutions." Paper presented at the Social Education Foundation Panel on Educational Opportunity and Postsecondary Desegregation, Austin, Tex., Feb. 10, 1994.

Rezler, A. G., and Rezmovic, V. "The Learning Preference Inventory." *Journal of Allied Health,* 1981, *10,* 28–34.

Sanchez, I. M. "An Analysis of Learning Style Constructs and the Development of a Profile of Hispanic Adult Learners." Unpublished doctoral dissertation, Department of Education, University of New Mexico, 1996.

Schmeck, R. R., Ribich, F., and Ramanaiah, N. "Development of a Self-Report Inventory for Assessing Differences in Learning Processes." *Allied Psychological Measurement,* 1977, *1,* 413–431.

Tierney, W. G. "Official Encouragement, Institutional Discouragement: Minorities in Academe." *The Native American Experience.* Norwood, N.J.: Ablex, 1994. (ED 413 117)

Tinto, V. *Leaving College: Rethinking the Causes and Cures of Student Attrition.* Chicago: University of Chicago Press, 1987.

Tinto, V. "Classrooms as Communities." *Journal of Higher Education,* 1997, *68*(6), 599–623.

Tinto, V. "Learning Communities: Building Gateways to Student Success." ACPA speech, St. Louis, Mo., 1999.

Trueba, H. T. "From Failure to Success: The Role of Culture and Culture Conflict in the Academic Achievement of Chicano Students." In R. R. Valencia (ed.), *Chicano School Failure and Success: Research and Policy Agenda for the 1990s.* Bristol, Pa.: Falmer Press, 1991. (ED 387 285)

U.S. Department of Education. "No More Excuses: The Final Report of the Hispanic Dropout Project." Report to Secretary Riley, U.S. Department of Education, Feb. 1998.

Weinstein, C. E. *LASSI Users Manual.* Clearwater, Fla.: H and H, 1987.

Witkin, H. A., Oltman, P. K., Reskin, E., and Karp, S. A. *A Manual for the Embedded Figures Test.* Palo Alto, Calif.: Consulting Psychologists Press, 1973.

IRENE M. SANCHEZ is director of the Health Careers Opportunities Program (HCOP) at Northern New Mexico Community College in Espanola, New Mexico. HCOP is a program designed to recruit minority students into the health professions.

4

Minority students often face greater challenges than their white peers in becoming integrated into the college environment. Recent research suggests that participation in a student success course could be especially beneficial for minority students who attend predominantly white community colleges. This chapter presents a model for designing and implementing a community college student success course.

Using Success Courses for Promoting Persistence and Completion

Martina Stovall

Students' diverse backgrounds, varying levels of commitment to earning a college degree, and numerous pressures from the external environment all influence their persistence in college. Regardless of the individual background characteristics, however, it is the students' daily interactions in the campus environment that have the greatest impact on their decision to stay in or leave college. The interactions believed to be the most critical in determining student persistence are those that occur within the first six months or first year of college (Tinto, 1994, 1996).

As new community college students begin to interact with others on campus, they develop a perception of how well they fit within the academic and social communities of the college. Students who perceive that they share common interests and academic abilities with other students and with faculty members feel a sense of integration in the college environment. The greater the sense of integration felt by students, the greater the likelihood that they will persist at the college until graduation. Students who fail to become integrated during the first year are more likely to leave college prior to graduation (Astin, 1984; Bean and Metzner, 1985; Tinto, 1975, 1993, 1996).

The wide diversity of community college students, with respect to high school experience, academic ability, social background, age, and career aspiration, makes integration more challenging (Astin, 1993). Many new community college students are not academically prepared for college-level courses and lack the necessary study strategies (Roueche and Roueche, 1993). Approximately 40 percent of the first-time freshmen enroll in at least one remedial course (American Association of Community Colleges, 1997).

NEW DIRECTIONS FOR COMMUNITY COLLEGES, no. 112, Winter 2000   © Jossey-Bass, a Wiley company

More than half of the students are the first in their family to attend college and are therefore often unfamiliar with the concepts and requirements of college (Gardner, 1996; London, 1996; Rendon, 1996). These students are more likely to be unsure about their educational goals and to rely on college personnel for help in planning their futures (Martens, Lara, Cordova, and Harris, 1995; Richardson and Elliott, 1994). Minority students often face greater challenges than their white peers in becoming integrated into the college environment. Many minority students not only enter college with characteristics that may hinder their academic success but also experience greater levels of social isolation and personal dissatisfaction than their white peers (McNairy, 1996; Pascarella and Terenzini, 1991).

Recognizing the challenges that many of their new students face, community colleges have implemented a variety of interventions aimed at facilitating students' integration into the college environment and improving their performance and persistence (Beal and Pascarella, 1982; Tinto, 1998). One specific intervention is the student success course, also referred to as the freshman seminar or extended orientation course (Barefoot and Fidler, 1996). Offering first-semester student success courses at community colleges is congruent with suggestions by Tinto (1990) and Pascarella and Terenzini (1991) that orientation activities should span the initial transition period of the first semester and help address students' needs as they arise.

Despite institutional variation in content and delivery, student success courses are generally offered with the overall goals of helping students identify campus resources, establish relationships with other students and with faculty members, and assess and improve their academic and life management skills (Barefoot and Fidler, 1996; Barefoot and Gardner, 1993). Numerous studies have shown positive relationships between participation in a student success course and academic performance and persistence (Barefoot and Gardner, 1993; Belcher, Ingold, and Lombard, 1987; Cuseo, 1991; Cuseo and Barefoot, 1996; Donnangelo and SantaRita, 1982; Glass and Garrett, 1995; Grunder and Hellmich, 1996; Smacchi, 1991; Walls, 1996).

One recent study (Stovall, 1999) suggests that participation in a student success course could be especially beneficial for minority students who attend predominantly white community colleges. The study was conducted at a Midwestern public rural community college with an annual enrollment of approximately five thousand students. Consistent with surrounding communities, there are few minorities in the college student body; approximately 97 percent of the students are classified as white, non-Hispanic. The study sample included 2,280 students who were divided into two groups based on first-term participation ($n = 97$) or nonparticipation ($n = 2183$) in a student success course. Consistent with the overall college student body, 3 percent of the nonparticipants were identified as minority. However, more than 15 percent of the participant group were identified as minority. The minority categories represented included African American,

Hispanic American, Indian American, A   gory of other ethnic minority.

Overall, the study confirmed the e   p between participation in a student succ   mance, persistence, and graduation. Whe   , success course participants earned high   grade point averages, completed greater percentages of their first-term credit hours, had greater odds of persisting to the second semester, second year, and third year, and had greater odds of graduating from the community college by the end of the three-year period following their initial enrollment. The researcher concluded that by aiding students' early integration into the college environment, enrollment in a success course had a positive impact on both their short-term and long-term academic performance and persistence.

Further examination revealed that enrollment in the course may have had a greater impact on the early success of minority students than on white students. When comparing the first-semester performance of the white success course participants with the white nonparticipants, participation in the course was associated with a .401 increase in first-term grade point average, $t(1929) = 3.525$, $p = .000$. When comparing the first-semester performance of the minority success course participants with the minority nonparticipants, participation in the course was associated with a .872 increase in first-term grade point average, $t(56) = 2.428$, $p = .039$.

The following model for designing and implementing a student success course is based on the course taught at the community college where this research was conducted. The course described, however, is typical of many offered at community colleges around the country today (Barefoot and Fidler, 1996).

Many issues must be considered in designing and implementing a student success course, including defining the goals of the course, determining the organization and delivery methods, developing the course content, gaining support on campus, recruiting and training instructors, recruiting students to enroll, and assessing the outcomes of the course (Jewler, 1989).

Goals of the Course

By helping first-semester students acquire the information, skills, attitudes, and behaviors needed for college success, the student success course facilitates their integration into both the academic and social communities of the college. Because many community college students have previously experienced limited academic success, one important goal of the student success course is to help them develop positive attitudes about learning and confidence in their abilities.

The student success course seeks to accommodate the needs and concerns of students of all ages with diverse educational backgrounds. The student success course provides a safe place for students to ask questions and discuss fears so that they can become secure in their new environment. The course introduces students to institutional resources and cocurricular opportunities. Ultimately, for both the students and the college, the student success course results in students' improved academic performance and increased retention.

Organization and Delivery

Decisions regarding the organization and delivery of the student success course provide a foundation on which to build course content. Three decisions regarding course organization and delivery are important: (1) determining the amount of credit to be awarded for the course, (2) determining class size, and (3) ensuring student contact with faculty members outside the classroom.

Awarding credit. Awarding graduation credit for a student success course validates the importance of the knowledge gained in the course. The course's reputation is often associated with the amount of credit awarded and the type of grading system used. In a 1994 national survey (Barefoot and Fidler, 1996), 84.1 percent of the responding community colleges reported that they award graduation credit for their student success courses. The majority of them (52.6 percent) award one hour of credit, 19.9 percent award two hours of credit, and 27.6 percent award three or more hours of credit. Most community colleges (83.8 percent) assign a letter grade for the course (Barefoot and Fidler, 1996). The student success course described in this chapter is a two-credit graded course that counts for elective credit toward graduation. As a two-credit-hour course, the course allows adequate time for ongoing, consistent contact throughout the entire first semester.

Class size and student interaction. Insufficient interaction with other students and with faculty members in college may lead to students' feelings of isolation (Tinto, 1996). Students may feel that they do not fit in at the college because they perceive a lack of support from other students and from faculty members. As mentioned previously, these feelings of isolation may lead to student withdrawal. Success course class sizes no larger than twenty-five students tend to promote interaction among the students and between the students and the course instructor. Class activities should involve group discussions and projects that are designed to assist students in establishing a supportive peer group. Through these group activities, students are also guided in becoming active participants in the learning process.

Faculty contact. Informal contact with faculty members outside the classroom can have a positive impact on students' feelings of support by the college (Astin, 1993; Tinto, 1994). The quality of these interactions with faculty members is more important than the quantity. Faculty-student interactions that focus on academic and career-related matters are believed to contribute most to students' persistence in college (Pascarella and Terenzini, 1991). All students enrolled in the student success course described in this chapter are required to meet individually with their success course instructor at least once early in the semester. The meetings are informal and students are encouraged to present questions or concerns about any aspect of college. The meetings generally focus on the students' academic and career plans. Although only one meeting is required, students are encouraged to meet with the course instructor throughout the semester. Often, student success course instructors informally serve as mentors to the course participants long after the students' first semesters.

Course Content

Similar to the overall design of student success courses described by Cuseo and Barefoot (1996), the student success course described in this chapter involves four major content areas: (1) introduction to college resources, (2) making the transition to college, (3) career development, and (4) life management. *★ formal requirement*

Introduction to college resources. The introduction to college resources is designed to help students locate and effectively use college resources. Students have the opportunity to learn important college policies and related dates. Class activities include an introduction to college publications and academic policies; a library tour; instruction in establishing an e-mail account; guest lectures on such college services as financial aid, career planning, and job placement; tutoring; academic advisement and registration; and student activities.

Making the transition to college. The content addressing the transition to college is designed to guide students in evaluating and improving their learning skills. Students explore their own learning stages and styles. They learn how memory works and the importance of organizing information and storing it according to how each one of us learns. Students learn skills to improve their abilities to focus and concentrate. They then apply this knowledge to learning in college—how to read college textbooks, how to take lecture notes, and how to study for tests. The content includes ongoing discussions regarding the differences between the academic and social demands of high school and college. Students also discuss how they can use the skills they are developing in college in their lives outside of college and in their careers after college graduation.

Career development. The course content on career development helps students develop career goals and identify and use resources available to assist with educational and career planning. Students learn to use a variety of instruments to evaluate their abilities, aptitudes, personalities, and interests, and then they relate these to the requirements of specific careers and college majors. Students develop a personal educational/career plan that includes research on at least one specific career and identification of an educational program that could lead to that career. Students use this information for planning course enrollment in future semesters at the college.

Life management. The life management content of the student success course includes development of time management, stress management, decision making, and relationship skills. Topics in this area are designed to help students develop strategies to effectively handle pressures in college and in life outside of college. They explore how much time they need to devote to attending classes and studying and how to better plan their course enrollment according to the time that they have available. This area of the course also seeks to help students improve communication in relationships and better understand and appreciate the similarities and differences among individuals.

All four major content areas are integrated throughout the course. By recognizing and discussing the evolution of a college semester and the common stages of college adjustment as they occur throughout the semester, students share common experiences and gain support from each other. For example, the career-planning segment of the course is completed near the registration period for courses in the second semester and is followed by information on academic advisement and registration. The student success course instructor helps ensure that the students have the resources and support needed for registration.

Gaining Support on Campus

Community college student success courses commonly originate and are organized through the student affairs division; however, as more departments become involved in the design and implementation of student success courses, the support for the courses will increase (Cuseo and Barefoot, 1996). Ongoing, campuswide collaboration involving administration, the faculty, and student affairs is essential in both the design and implementation of the course.

Sharing the results of research describing the benefits of student success courses can foster campus support. This can be especially helpful if the research can be related to current concerns on campus, such as student retention. It is helpful to stress not only how student success courses can benefit students but also how they can benefit the institution. Classroom instructors benefit when students come to class better prepared for college-level work. The entire institution benefits when students are successful and retention is improved.

Recruiting and Training Instructors

Ideally, community college student success courses are taught by a combination of instructors, student affairs professionals, and administrators. It is recommended that those who teach the course be full-time college staff members so that they are available on campus when student concerns arise throughout the first semester. It is critical that success course instructors possess the needed expertise, credentials, and dedication to teach the course. Only those instructors who want to teach a student success course should do so, and they should be provided adequate time for course preparation and individual contact with students. The content and process of the success course will demand provision of frequent and thorough instructor guidance and feedback.

Approximately 70 percent of the community colleges that offer student success courses offer some type of instructor training (Barefoot and Fidler, 1996). At the community college described in this chapter, all instructors are required to participate in training prior to teaching the course for the first time. The initial training, led by the more experienced success course instructors on campus, not only develops instructor understanding of the goals, content, and processes of the course but also allows instructors to interact and develop relationships with one another. Having the more experienced success course instructors share their best practices and learning experiences is invaluable for new instructors.

All of the student success course instructors participate in ongoing professional development opportunities that emphasize developing classroom activities and techniques that promote student involvement and learning. The ongoing training is also used to maintain the instructors' current awareness of campus activities and events.

Recruiting Students to Enroll

According to the 1994 national survey previously mentioned (Barefoot and Fidler, 1996), 26.8 percent of the community colleges that offer a student success course require it for all new students. An additional 37.3 percent require it for some students (Barefoot and Fidler, 1996). In order to provide an opportunity for all community college students to benefit from enrollment in a success course, community college administrators should ensure that an adequate number of sections of the course are offered at times convenient to students.

Community college students should be advised of the potential benefits of participation in a success course. These potential benefits should be discussed during orientation activities prior to student registration for the first term, and all new students should be encouraged to enroll. Enrollment should be highly recommended, if not required, for community college students who are assessed as lacking college-level academic skills. Awarding graduation credit for the course will reduce student resistance and will validate the importance of the course.

High school counselors and community college advisors, counselors, and instructors should be well informed of the positive impact of participation in a success course on student performance, persistence, and graduation. Advisors and counselors can use the information to encourage students to enroll in a success course during their first term in college.

College instructors can use the information to refer students who are experiencing difficulties during the first semester to a success course.

Community colleges can encourage enrollment in student success courses by integrating the courses into the first-semester core curriculum of academic programs that have a high rate of student departure prior to graduation. The program faculty members teaching the course could relate the academic study skills component of the success course to the content of other required first-semester courses.

Assessing Outcomes

Continuous assessment of the outcomes of participation in a student success course should be conducted at each college to make certain that the course is achieving the desired outcomes for that particular college. Needed course revisions and improvements can then be determined according to the assessment results. As the needs of community college students continue to change, so too will the needs of student success course participants. It is imperative that community colleges continuously monitor and adjust the content and delivery of their student success courses to meet the needs of their students. The outcomes of student success courses most frequently measured at community colleges are student satisfaction with course and instructor, use of campus services, and student satisfaction with the institution (Barefoot and Gardner, 1993).

Conclusion

Tinto (1994) suggested that the first six months of college are the most critical in determining whether or not a student will become integrated into the academic and social communities of a college. Minority students who attend predominantly white colleges face greater challenges in becoming integrated than their white peers. Enrollment in a student success course can help these students become integrated during that first six months. Research has shown that enrollment in a student success course is associated with higher first-term grade point averages, higher first-term credit hour completion, greater odds of continuing enrollment until the second term, second year, or third year of college and greater odds of graduating. Providing student success courses indicates to students the college's willingness to make student success a priority.

Effective development of a community college student success course demands campuswide efforts and involves many considerations. This chapter provides one model that can be used to guide that process. For more information on establishing a student success course, see Gardner (1989), Barefoot and Gardner (1993), and Kenny (1996).

References

American Association of Community Colleges. *National Profile of Community Colleges: Trends and Statistics 1997–1998.* Washington, D.C.: American Association of Community Colleges, 1997.

Astin, A. W. "Student Involvement: A Developmental Theory for Higher Education." *Journal of College Student Personnel,* 1984, 25(4), 297–308.

Astin, A. W. *What Matters in College? Four Critical Years Revisited.* San Francisco: Jossey-Bass, 1993.

Barefoot, B. O., and Gardner, J. N. "The Freshman Orientation Seminar: Extending the Benefits of Traditional Orientation." In M. L. Upcraft and others, *Designing Successful Transitions: A Guide for Orienting Students to College.* National Resource Center for the Freshman Year Experience, Division of Continuing Education, no. 13. Columbia: University of South Carolina, 1993, pp. 141–153.

Barefoot, B. O., and Fidler, P. P. *The National Survey of Freshman Seminar Programs: Continuing Innovations in the Collegiate Curriculum.* Columbia, S. C.: National Resource Center for the Freshman Year Experience and Students in Transition, 1996.

Beal, P., and Pascarella, E. T. "Designing Retention Interventions and Verifying Their Effectiveness." In E. T. Pascarella (ed.), *Studying Student Attrition.* New Directions for Institutional Research, no. 36. San Francisco: Jossey-Bass, 1982.

Bean, J. P., and Metzner, B. S. "A Conceptual Model of Nontraditional Undergraduate Student Attrition. *Review of Educational Research,* 1985, 55(4), 485–540.

Belcher, M. J., Ingold, S., and Lombard, M. *Addressing Retention Through an Orientation Course: Results from a North Campus Study.* Research Report No. 87-24. Miami: Miami-Dade Community College, 1987. (ED 296 761)

Cuseo, J. B. *The Freshman Orientation Seminar: A Research-Based Rationale for Its Value, Delivery, and Content.* Columbia, S. C.: National Resource Center for the Freshman Year Experience and Students in Transition, 1991.

Cuseo, J. B., and Barefoot, B. O. "A Natural Marriage: The Extended Orientation Seminar and the Community College." In J. N. Hankin (ed.), *The Community College: Opportunity and Access for America's First-Year Students.* Columbia, S. C.: National Resource Center for the Freshman Year Experience and Students in Transition, 1996.

Donnangelo, F. P., and Santa Rita, E. D. *The Effects of Two College Orientation Courses upon the Academic Performance and Retention of Entering Freshmen.* Unpublished manuscript, Bronx Community College, New York, 1982. (ED 232 747)

Gardner, J. N. "Starting a Freshman Seminar Program." In M. L. Upcraft and J. N. Gardner (eds.), *The Freshman Year Experience: Helping Students Survive and Succeed in College.* San Francisco: Jossey-Bass, 1989.

Gardner, J. N. "Helping America's First-Generation College Students." *About Campus,* 1996, 1(5), 31–32.

Glass, J. C. Jr., and Garrett, M. S. "Student Participation in a College Orientation Course, Retention, and Grade Point Average." *Community College Journal of Research and Practice,* 1995, 19, 117–132.

Grunder, P. G., and Hellmich, D. M. "Academic Persistence and Achievement of Remedial Students in a Community College's College Success Program." *Community College Review,* 1996, 24(2), 21–33.

Jewler, A. J. "Elements of an Effective Seminar: The University 101 Program." In J. L. Upcraft and J. N. Gardner (eds.), *The Freshman Year Experience: Helping New Students Survive and Succeed in College.* San Francisco: Jossey-Bass, 1989.

Kenny, D. A. "The Politics of Creating and Maintaining a College Success Course." In J. N. Hankin (ed.), *The Community College: Opportunity and Access for America's First-Year Students.* National Resource Center for the Freshman Year Experience, no. 19. Columbia: University of South Carolina, 1996, pp. 69–76.

London, H. B. "How College Affects First-Generation College Students." *About Campus,* 1996, *1*(5), 9–13, 23.

Martens, K., Lara, E., Cordova, J., and Harris, H. "Community College Students: Ever Changing, Ever New." In S. R. Helfgot and M. M. Culp (eds.), *Promoting Student Success in the Community College.* New Directions for Student Services, no. 69. San Francisco: Jossey-Bass, 1995.

McNairy, F. G. "The Challenge for Higher Education: Retaining Students of Color." In I. H. Johnson and A. J. Ottens (eds.), *Leveling the Playing Field: Promoting Academic Success for Students of Color.* New Directions for Student Services, no. 74. San Francisco: Jossey-Bass, 1996.

Pascarella, E. T., and Terenzini, P. T. *How College Affects Students: Findings and Insights from Twenty Years of Research.* San Francisco: Jossey-Bass, 1991.

Rendon, L. I. "Life on the Border." *About Campus,* 1996, *1*(5), 14–20.

Richardson, R. C., Jr., and Elliott, D. B. "Improving Opportunities for Underprepared Students." In T. O'Banion (ed.), *Teaching and Learning in the Community College.* Washington, D.C.: American Association of Community Colleges, 1994.

Roueche, J. E., and Roueche, S. D. *Between a Rock and a Hard Place: The At-Risk Student in the Open-Door College.* Washington, D.C.: American Association of Community Colleges, 1993.

Smacchi, L. A. "Evaluating a Freshman Orientation Course at a Community College." Doctoral dissertation, Temple University. *Dissertation Abstracts International,* 1991, 52(07), 2382A.

Stovall, M. L. "Relationships Between Participation in a Community College Student Success Course and Academic Performance and Persistence." Unpublished doctoral dissertation, University of Illinois, Urbana-Champaign, 1999.

Tinto, V. "Dropout from Higher Education: A Theoretical Synthesis of Recent Research." *Review of Educational Research,* 1975, *45*(1), 89–125.

Tinto, V. "Principles of Effective Retention." *Journal of the Freshman Year Experience,* 1990, 2(1), 35–48.

Tinto, V. *Leaving College: Rethinking the Causes and Cures of Student Attrition.* (2nd ed.) Chicago: University of Chicago Press, 1994.

Tinto, V. "Persistence and First-Year Experience at the Community College: Teaching New Students to Survive, Stay and Thrive." In J. N. Hankin (ed.), *The Community College: Opportunity and Access from America's First-Year Students.* Columbia, S. C.: National Resource Center for the Freshman Year Experience and Students in Transition, 1996.

Tinto, V. "Colleges as Communities: Taking Research on Student Persistence Seriously." *Review of Higher Education,* 1998, *21*(2), 167–177.

Walls, G. D. "An Evaluation of an Orientation to College Course in a Community College Setting." (Doctoral dissertation, University of Illinois). *Dissertation Abstracts International,* 1996, 57(8), 3372A.

When this article was written, MARTINA STOVALL *was director of counseling at Lake Land College, Mattoon, Illinois. She is now dean of counseling, advising, and minority student affairs at Moraine Valley Community College in Palos Hills, Illinois.*

5

Increasing retention and success for minority students through mentoring is the focus of this chapter. A model for a formal mentoring program, AMIGOS™, is discussed with details for implementation.

Increasing Retention and Success Through Mentoring

Linda K. Stromei

Whether driven by the American ideal of justice or by legal mandates, the community college, with its open-door policy, is most likely to interact with (and hence be responsible for) the student at risk. To help ensure the success of these graduates, community colleges must offer training that is job-specific as well as guidance to assist graduates in their transition from school to work. Mentoring programs are increasingly being used to provide this help. Mentoring programs at community colleges are also well suited to increasing the retention of those students who are typically at risk, the minority students.

Traditionally, mentoring in academic settings has focused on learning rather than career development or psychosocial needs (Ensher, 1997; Stromei, 1998). By focusing on work-based learning, community colleges can move away from the educational paradigm of knowledge acquisition, which often ignores knowledge application. Hoerner and Wehrley (1995) define work-based learning as "the knowledge/learning imparted to every student from the beginning of schooling which maintains a theme or focus that people work to live and that there is a positive connectedness between the schooling process and living productive lives" (p. xiii).

Hoerner and Wehrley (1995) found that America has the worst school-to-work transition of any industrialized nation in the world. Mentoring that combines learning and doing can help students to better make the transition from school to work. Providing students with a mentor at both school and work increases the likelihood of success at both locations and can contribute to a smooth transition to the postsecondary environment and eventually to the workplace.

NEW DIRECTIONS FOR COMMUNITY COLLEGES, no. 112, Winter 2000   © Jossey-Bass, a Wiley company

Most of the Fortune 500 companies report some type of formal mentoring program, recognizing the value of mentoring for the growth and success of employees. Companies are discovering that few mentoring relationships develop spontaneously and are implementing formal programs to nurture all their promising employees. Many companies are using mentoring programs to promote ethnic and gender diversity. Sheehy (1977) and Kanter (1977) reported on the importance of mentors for women. "Almost without exception, the women I studied who did gain recognition in their careers were at some point nurtured by a mentor" (Sheehy, 1977). Kanter reported that women who failed were without a support system or mentors to provide sponsorship.

A mentor can provide not only job-specific knowledge and training but also valuable insight into an organization's environment and culture, as well as psychosocial support for the student.

Mentoring Minority Students in the Community College

Mentoring can take several forms in the community college. Students can participate in internships, cooperative education, and apprenticeships. These programs are a part of all community college curricula. However, a mentoring component is not always inherent in these programs. Often it is left up to the individual student or his or her supervisor to develop a mentoring relationship. A more effective form, particularly for the minority student, is a formal, facilitated mentoring program.

The community college needs to take a proactive role to ensure that these programs include a mentoring component. Research has shown that community colleges are recognizing this need and are strengthening the mentoring role in their school-to-work programs (Price, Graham, and Hobbs, 1997). Price, Graham, and Hobbs discuss the need for specific programs at community colleges to train both the school and the work-based mentors. Too often, the school assumes that the organization will take care of that aspect, while the organization assumes that it is the school's role to provide everything.

With blacks, Hispanics, and Native Americans continuing to be underrepresented in higher education and the professions, it behooves community colleges to improve the retention opportunities for these underrepresented groups. Institutions can help eliminate barriers to retention by addressing the issues surrounding academic preparedness of minority students, exploring the extent of financial assistance to those students desiring an education, and fostering a positive educational climate. A formal mentoring program specifically designed for these students is one way to foster a positive educational climate.

In their 1997 study, Reichert and Absher compiled the opinions of a variety of scholars in defining salient issues affecting minority students.

Their list includes inadequate academic preparation, substandard educational resources, mismatched social and academic expectations, lack of encouragement, psychological intimidation, unstable familial and financial circumstances, inadequate peer support, lack of role modeling and mentoring, and so on. The researchers listed a mentoring program among the many strategies for improving the retention of these minority students.

Beatty-Guenter (1994) proposes a typology of retention strategies for minority at-risk students. This typology clarifies the commonalities in various retention strategies and thus provides a framework for research and practice. The four types of retention strategies are (1) sorting students into homogeneous subgroups, (2) supporting students in dealing with life's problems or responsibilities, (3) connecting students with one another and with the institution, and (4) transforming students and the community college.

The supporting strategies Beatty-Guenter (1994) identifies are things that help to ease students' problems with aspects of everyday life. They include but are not limited to assistance in dealing with finances, home and family, transportation, on-campus day care, financial aid, parking and transportation, campus security arrangements, and college health and wellness programs. Attrition studies have shown that students at community colleges most often drop out because of the pressures of meeting the challenges of everyday life. A trained mentor is well equipped to assist a student with these everyday problems.

The connecting strategy is designed to promote bonding between the student and the institution. This attachment often promotes a sense of community that in turn motivates the student to remain enrolled at the college. Well-designed school-based mentoring programs provide the social and academic integration and involvement that are critical to ensuring the retention and academic achievement of students at risk. The inability of most minority community college students to participate in traditional college activities places them at risk. Connecting with a mentor on a psychosocial level provides support and encouragement to bridge this participation gap.

Mentoring programs are also a successful strategy for connecting the student with college representatives, other students, and community members. A major element in a retention program for black, Hispanic, Native American, and Asian students at Prince George's Community College is individual support provided by mentors. The mentors are drawn from the college's full-time and part-time faculty, staff, and administrators. The matching and mentor training focuses on developing positive relationships with minority students. Workshop training has also emphasized fostering supportive classroom environments, as well as appropriate support-service referrals, for minority students (James, 1991).

In his 1991 study, James evaluated the program's impact on minorities and examined differences in retention between two groups of black students—those who participated in the mentoring program and those who did not. He also evaluated the differences in retention between members of the black participant group and white students at the college who did not participate in the program. The findings indicate that 66 percent of the black students in the participant group successfully completed 100 percent of their credit courses—a percentage equal to that of the first-time, degree-seeking white comparison group. In the black nonparticipant group, 51 percent of the students completed 100 percent of their credit courses. Eighty percent of the participant group returned to the college in the spring semester. In contrast, 73 percent of the black nonparticipant group and 83 percent of the white comparison returned.

Northeast Illinois University (NEIU), which boasts a minority population of 54 percent, has a minority student mentoring program known as "Partners for Success." The goals of this program are to guide students in learning the ropes at NEIU, develop a plan for both their academic and career success, and enrich their personal growth through contact with a mentor. Research conducted over the past five years indicates that there is a measurable positive correlation between the students' participation in the mentoring program and their persistence in their degree program—that is, student retention (Kelly and Llacuna, 2000).

Mentoring programs that acknowledge the academic and vocational aspects of the community college experience have proven effective in improving minority students' academic performance and retention rates. A model that incorporates successful elements of mentoring programs of the past can be applied in community college settings to address the unique needs of minority students.

The Importance of Tacit Knowledge

The key benefit of mentoring programs is to provide the opportunity to transfer critical knowledge to the next generation of workers. Organizations today face a knowledge drain with the impending retirement of many baby boomers within the next five to seven years. Much of the knowledge these workers possess is tacit knowledge, which cannot can be learned from a book, or even at school. And the students who gain this tacit knowledge will have an advantage in the workplace of tomorrow. Mentoring is the method used to transfer this tacit knowledge, and because minorities do not participate in mentoring programs as often as nonminorities, they are at a disadvantage to fill these jobs.

Engstrom (forthcoming) has described tacit knowledge as indefinable, indeterminate, strictly personal, and related to human knowledge; at the same time, it involves more than we can articulate. "A person performing a somersault serves as a good illustration of tacit knowledge. Thinking hard about every movement before the jump, the person will most likely fail. Neither if the somersault is successful will the person be able to explain in detail how it was performed. The trick is to internalize the movement so that the body does it automatically. It is then possible to say that the athlete has a tacit knowledge about how to perform the somersault."

Nonaka and Takeuchi (1995) identify the points belonging to the tacit dimension of knowledge as follows:

- Not easily visible and expressible
- Highly personal
- Deeply rooted in the actions, experiences, ideas, values, and emotions of a person
- Hard to formalize
- Difficult to communicate and share with others
- Subjective insights, intuitions, and hunches

They further divide tacit knowledge into two dimensions—technical and cognitive. The technical dimension consists of skills, crafts, and expertise otherwise known as "know-how." Mental processes and intellect make up the cognitive dimension. Furthermore, it can be seen as a person's "image of reality and vision for the future."

Finally, tacit knowledge can be hard to pinpoint, and it mainly involves the capacity of the human brain. It can be thought of as the knowledge of one's experiences.

The process of socialization relies on experience in knowledge acquisition. This experience creates tacit knowledge, which can take the form of mental models or technical skills. Language as a communication tool is not necessary in the process of socialization. Tacit knowledge can be transformed via observation, imitation, and practice. A student paired with an older, more experienced student would gain the tacit knowledge of the older student—skills that would improve the retention of the younger student.

A mentor can serve two functions for a protégé: career-related and psychosocial. The career-related function includes providing sponsorship, exposure, visibility, coaching, protection, and challenging assignments that directly relate to the career development of the protégé. The psychosocial function includes providing role modeling, acceptance, confirmation, counseling, and friendship—socialization activities that influence the protégé's self-image (Chao, Walz, and Gardner, 1992).

Tacit knowledge is transferred from mentor to protégé, which can be done in several ways. The experience needs to come alive for the protégé via oral stories, written documents such as letters and e-mails, videos, and observation. The AMIGOS™ formal mentoring program provides opportunities for mentors to be trained in the transfer of knowledge via several methods and for the protégés to be trained in proactive techniques designed to improve the mentoring relationship.

The AMIGOS™ Formal Mentoring Model

Conceptualized as a result of numerous years of research on mentoring programs nationwide, the AMIGOS™ model (Stromei, 1998) is currently being used in numerous organizations nationwide. One implementation is with an intern program at Sandia National Laboratories in Albuquerque, New Mexico. Developed in conjunction with Sandia's knowledge management program, the intern program pairs a young scientist or engineer with an older, more experienced professional for a two-year program of intense study and application. Minorities and women are well represented in the intern group.

AMIGOS™ is an acronym for Arranged Mentor for Instructional Guidance and Organizational (or Other) Support. It is a model for a formal mentoring program in an organization or educational setting. The model focuses on both the mentor and the protégé, together interacting with the four centers of the model:

1. *The IDEA (Individual Diagnosis, Evaluation, and Assessment) center.* A profile of the mentor and protégé is prepared to assist the program facilitator with matching. Assessment instruments are used to identify personality type and other characteristics of the pairs. Studies indicate greater student success with a teacher of similar personality type. An assessment of the student's skills is used to match the student with a mentor who can provide the needed skills. Interviews with previous mentoring pairs indicate that those pairs with the greatest satisfaction and highest skills transfer develop a rapport at the beginning of their relationship. One young Asian protégé reports, "My mentor and I connected on our first meeting, and every time we met we would discover more things we had in common. I don't think I would have been willing to share my problems with him if I didn't feel that connection and trust" (Stromei, 1998).

2. *The TIPS (Training Instruction Practical Tips) center.*

3. *The COPE (Center for Organizational Problem Enlightenment).* A problem-based activity pairs the mentor and protégé together in the COPE. In an organization, these activities are often based on a current work project. It is during these problem-based activities that the student is able to observe, imitate, and practice. The pairs move to the TIPS center, where they receive training, suggestions for classes and assignments, and other available resources necessary for them to succeed.

4. *The FUN (Friendship, Understanding, and Nurturing) center.* To jumpstart the socialization and rapport that is an essential part of mentoring, the pairs meet in a retreat or other social setting, which takes place in the FUN center of the model. School-based mentors attend school functions with their student protégés while the work-based mentors arrange outside lunches and other social activities. A young Hispanic protégé expressed his pleasure at visiting his mentor's home for a weekend barbecue. "He has welcomed me into his family. Having this relationship has really made a difference for me."

The initial length of this model for a formal mentoring program is one year, but it is recommended that it be renewed for an additional year. For students, the ideal would be the entire time they are enrolled at the community college, and, ideally, one or both of the mentors could stay with the student during the student's transition to the postsecondary learning environment. The literature reveals that mentoring results are often not seen in the first year. Some protégés report feeling that the program is ending just when they are really getting to know their mentor. The activities of this model—particularly the retreat/social in the beginning and the problem-based learning—are designed to shorten the learning or acquaintance curve for the pairs and give the relationship a jump start.

Evaluation is an important component to the program facilitators and participants, especially the anecdotal data obtained from the students. Although strong quantitative data results are available for the organizational implementations of this model (Stromei, 1998, 1999), the intern evaluation data are still in the preliminary stages. Anecdotal data at the three-, six-, and nine-month reviews are positive and indicate high satisfaction among both mentors and protégés. These data are consistent with those of other researchers in higher education and indicate that the formal mentoring program has at least some elevating impact on the retention rates of minority students.

References

Beatty-Guenter, P. "Sorting, Supporting, Connecting, and Transforming: Retention Strategies at Community Colleges." *Community College Journal of Research and Practice,* 1994, *18*(2), 113–129.

Chao, G. T., Walz, P. M., and Gardner, P. D. "Formal and Informal Mentorships: A Comparison of Mentoring Functions and Contrast with Nonmentored Counterparts." *Personnel Psychology,* 1992, *45*, 619–636.

Engstrom, T. "Knowledge Mentoring in Practice." In L. K. Stromei (ed.), *Promoting Life-Long Learning Through Mentoring and Coaching, in Action.* Alexandria, Va.: American Society for Training and Development Press, forthcoming.

Ensher, E. A. "The Effect of Social Exchanges on Diverse Mentoring Relationships and Career Outcomes." Unpublished doctoral dissertation, Claremont Graduate University, 1997.

Hoerner, J. L., and Wehrley, J. B. *Work-Based Learning: The Key to School-to-Work Transition.* New York: McGraw-Hill, 1995.

James, D. P. "Minority Student Retention: The Prince George's Community College Program." In D. Angel and A. Barrera (eds.), *Rekindling Minority Enrollment.* New Directions for Community Colleges, no. 74. San Francisco: Jossey-Bass, 1991.

Kanter, R. M. *Men and Women of the Corporation.* New York: Basic Books, 1977.

Kelly, M. T., and Llacuna, F. "Can Involvement in a Mentoring Program Affect Enrollment Persistence for Minority Students?" *The Mentoring Connection,* Summer 2000, pp. 1–3.

Nonaka, I., and Takeuchi, H. *The Knowledge-Creating Company.* New York: Oxford University Press, 1995.

Price, C., Graham, C., and Hobbs, J. "Workplace Mentoring: Considerations and Exemplary Practices." In E. I. Farmer and C. B. Key (eds.), *School-to-Work Systems: The Role of Community Colleges in Preparing Students and Facilitating Transitions.* New Directions for Community Colleges, no. 97. San Francisco: Jossey-Bass, 1997.

Reichert, M., and Absher, M. "Taking Another Look at Educating African American Engineers: The Importance of Undergraduate Retention." *Journal of Engineering Education*, 1997, *86*, 241–253.

Sheehy, G. *Passages: Predictable Crises of Adult Life.* New York: NAL/Dutton, 1977.

Stromei, L. K. "An Evaluation of a Formal Mentoring Program for Managers, and the Determinants for Protégé Satisfaction." Unpublished doctoral dissertation, University of New Mexico, 1998.

Stromei, L. K. "Training Today's Leaders with Yesterday's Techniques." In F. C. Ashby (ed.), *Effective Leadership Programs, in Action.* Alexandria, Va.: American Society for Training and Development Press, 1999.

LINDA KYLE STROMEI is president of LINCO, LLC, a consulting firm that is the exclusive distributor of the AMIGOS™ mentoring program. She is also coordinator of the Teaching Assistant Resource Center at the University of New Mexico, Albuquerque, and serves on the board of directors of the International Mentoring Association.

6

When Middlesex Community College opened two new campuses in 1987, the student development staff recognized the importance of recruiting and retaining a new student population of largely Southeast Asian and Hispanic immigrants. A multifaceted program—which included curriculum changes, new student organizations, and orientation activities—was developed to create a more inclusive campus environment.

Creating a Campus Climate in Which Diversity Is Truly Valued

Evelyn Clements

This chapter describes a series of initiatives that Middlesex Community College undertook to create a campus climate in which students truly value differences in others and appreciate cultural diversity. To address a major shift in student demographics, the student development staff created a series of initiatives that would change the campus climate and infuse the value of cultural diversity throughout the college community. We wanted to create programs that could be sustained over a period of time and that would not be dependent on limited or transitory budget factors. Our specific objectives included expanding student services that support cultural diversity and global awareness through personal, professional, curricular, and campus development. These objectives were developed at college-wide meetings that included administrators and faculty and staff members. Throughout our planning, we wanted to emphasize collaboration with other departments and areas of the college.

The program's seven key initiatives are to (1) change the focus of the orientation program to emphasize the importance of valuing diversity, (2) develop an easy-access program for English-as-a-Second-Language (ESL) students, (3) revise a portion of the student activities budget to focus on programs that address issues of diversity, (4) develop opportunities for students to experience different cultures by creating international student fellowships, (5) create an international club on campus, (6) integrate the appreciation of cultural differences into the Freshman Seminar curriculum, and (7) develop a student improvisational theater troupe. These initiatives were implemented using current staff members and reallocating existing funds. Additional funds were used to hire part-time faculty members in the

New Directions for Community Colleges, no. 112, Winter 2000   © Jossey-Bass, a Wiley company

easy-access ESL program (Prepare to Attend College) and to provide a modest stipend for the student actors in the theater troupe.

Two Campuses, Many Cultures

The college has gone through tremendous changes in the last ten years, which have created serious yet exciting challenges for the student development staff. Middlesex Community College was originally founded in 1970 in Bedford, Massachusetts, a suburban community twenty miles northwest of Boston, and it occupied quarters at a Veterans Administration hospital. As the college grew over the years, it expanded to include additional temporary sites in the surrounding Bedford area.

In 1987, Middlesex opened a campus in Lowell, Massachusetts, and the plan for the next five years was that Middlesex would evolve into two permanent campuses: one in Bedford and one in Lowell. The opening of the Lowell campus occurred when the city of Lowell was experiencing intense growth that was creating great stress within the city. There was a huge influx of Southeast Asians who settled in Lowell during the 1980s, resulting in the largest population of Southeast Asians in the United States outside of Long Beach, California. In addition, a substantial number of Hispanics were living in Lowell. Youth gangs became a problem in the city, and racial tensions were high. When the college opened in Lowell, the Lowell public schools were admitting up to 250 new Southeast Asian students per week, and the dropout rate for minority students at Lowell High School was dramatic. As the Middlesex campus opened in Lowell, it was critical for the college to establish a campus climate that encouraged harmony among students of different cultures and backgrounds.

The student population at the Middlesex campus in Lowell grew very quickly, from 392 students in 1987—with 75 Hispanics and 25 Southeast Asians—to 2,547 students by 1994—25 percent of whom were minorities. The largest groups of minority students were Southeast Asians and Hispanics, but there were substantial numbers of students representing other countries throughout the world.

At about the same time the Lowell campus was opening, the Bedford campus, located twelve miles south of Lowell, was fortunate enough to receive funding for a new permanent campus, which opened in 1992. Students at the Bedford campus were primarily from surrounding suburban towns northwest of Boston. They were generally first-generation college students, and only about 9 percent were minorities. The vast majority of students in Bedford had limited experience with other cultures, and according to faculty and staff members, many of these students were not tolerant of those who were different from them. By 1993, both campuses had an equal number of students that totaled approximately seven thousand.

The Challenge

The challenge for the college and for the student development staff during this period of change was enormous. How could we set a tone that created racial harmony and encouraged students from different cultures to appreciate one another? How could we ensure that both campuses would be viewed equally so that one was not considered a "minority" campus and the other a "majority" campus? How could we encourage tolerance among students at the Bedford campus, when they had so little exposure to other races and cultures? And how could we be sure that racial and cultural tensions would not develop at the Lowell campus, where there was such a mix of students? The challenge was compounded by the fact that these were extremely difficult fiscal times, with little if any chance of bringing in additional staff members. Although funding was available to build and purchase new campuses, there was virtually no funding available to provide new support services. We had to design programs with the resources we had.

There developed early on a consensus of opinion that helped establish a foundation for our initiatives in student development. First, we agreed that neither campus should be viewed as primary and that whatever initiatives we developed should be carried out at both campuses. Every student at Middlesex needed to understand and accept the importance of valuing diversity, regardless of which campus he or she attended. Second, the importance of valuing diversity had to be seen as the primary goal, and our initiatives had to be visible and continually emphasized. Third, we had to provide opportunities for our students to see and experience different cultures. Unless we provided those opportunities, many students would never have that chance. Fourth, we wanted to provide substantive programs. Offering such activities as international festivals that featured foods from different countries would not be enough. Finally, members of the student development staff had to collaborate with all other members of the college community in achieving these goals. It must be added that the president saw this as a very high priority, and her leadership encouraged the development of new initiatives across all areas of the college.

A Multifaceted Program

This program consists of a series of initiatives (introduced at the beginning of the chapter) that were created by staff members within student development, often in collaboration with other areas of the college. These seven initiatives were all developed within the last seven years, and we keep them all active in our effort to sustain belief in the value of cultural diversity on our campus. This program has received the Region I Exemplary Program Award from the National Council on Student Development (an affiliate council of the American Association of Community Colleges) and it was honored by a third-place award as an outstanding program in student development at the Interassociation Conference (NASPA, NCSD, and ACPA) in Dallas, Texas, in 1995. Following is a discussion of each of our seven initiatives:

1. *Change the focus of the orientation program to emphasize the importance of valuing diversity.* We agreed that if valuing diversity was the most important value to emphasize to our students, then they needed to hear that during their first official day at the college. Our orientation program occurs for one day just before classes begin. We have eliminated all opening remarks from speakers, with the exception of a brief welcoming message by the president. Instead, we invite a faculty member, followed by a student, to give a keynote address about what valuing differences means to him or her. Almost always, the faculty member belongs to a minority group, and often, the speeches are deeply moving. Some faculty members speak about their own experiences with prejudice; others talk about the impact diversity has had in their lives. The students listen intently, and many have commented about what an impact those speeches have had on them. We emphasize the same theme every year, because our values remain consistent.

In addition, we know that visual symbols are important in making a statement to students about our values, so student government offered to purchase flags representing the countries of origin of our students. These flags are displayed in the cafeteria at the Bedford and Lowell campuses, and each year at the commencement exercises, the flags are carried first as the line of march begins. These flags are a source of pride for our students.

2. *Develop an easy-access program to recruit students from the community.* We have found that many people in the Lowell community, particularly those with English language problems or those who were new to the country, were uncertain about higher education. They were often afraid to begin. We developed a six-week beginning and intermediate ESL program (no credit) that is free of charge to anyone in the community. The program is offered approximately three times per year, and about 150 students participate in the program annually. Any given group has students from as many as fifteen different countries who vary in age from eighteen to sixty-five. With the help of a currently enrolled staff member, these students bond with one another, which is evident during the graduation ceremony when each member of the class cooks a traditional dish from his or her country of origin and invites members of the college community to participate in enjoying the food and traditional dance.

This program encourages nonnative English speakers from the community who might not otherwise think of going to college to give the college experience a try at no cost. The support and encouragement they receive serves as a catalyst for them to enter the college. The actual cost to the college, aside from the time of the staff member who spends a part of his or her time supporting these students, involves only the cost of the part-time faculty members who teach these sections and are very devoted to the program. The college, in turn, develops a group of students who have formed support systems and are ready to begin college.

3. *Revise a portion of the student activities budget to focus on programs that address issues of diversity.* If we want to emphasize the importance of diversity, we had better continue that theme throughout the students' experience at the college. The associate dean of student development, in collaboration with the Bedford and Lowell student planning boards for student activities, has redirected some activities funds and has developed a series called "The One World Series: A Community at Work." Each semester, a full series of programs and activities that address issues of diversity are presented in a colorful brochure that is distributed to the faculty, staff, and students. Faculty members often work collaboratively with the student life office and suggest speakers and programs for this series, and many bring their classes to the events. The dean of the social science division has been so impressed with the series that she has encouraged faculty members in her division to ask that students attend the series as a part of their course work. Recent speakers have included Marjorie Agosin, speaking on gender and human rights in Latin America, and Philip Permutter, speaking on bigotry in America. Each semester the series includes various types of activities, including music, lectures, and other events—all of which emphasize the theme of valuing differences.

4. *Develop opportunities for students to experience different cultures by creating international student fellowships.* We knew that many of our students had never been outside the United States; some, in fact, had never even been outside Massachusetts. How could our students begin to experience different cultures and customs when most could not afford to travel extensively? The student government was strongly in favor of creating opportunities to expose students to new cultures, and after some lengthy discussion, they enthusiastically agreed to discontinue a major program they had previously funded and instead set aside funds that could be used as fellowships for international study. These funds became a permanent component of the student activities budget, and as a result, the international fellowship program was created.

The fellowship program consists of three three-credit courses involving a series of lectures about the culture, history, and customs of a particular country, along with a trip to visit that country. Under the fellowships, we have sent ten students along with two faculty advisors over the past seven years on study opportunities to China, Europe, and most recently Costa Rica. All expenses, including travel, food, and lodging, are covered either by the fellowship funds or by arrangement with the host country. The students pay for only their passport, visa, incidental expenses, and the cost of enrolling in a standard three-credit course.

These fellowship opportunities have virtually changed students' lives. Some of the students selected have never been on an airplane before. One student had lived for a while with her children in a shelter for battered women and had never been beyond the Lowell/Boston area. Some students have decided to focus on international relations as a result of participating in this program. Two of the students who had participated in one of the first fellowships to China have recently graduated from Tufts University with a special interest in international relations. Before attending Middlesex, one of them had been a full-time chef and the other had run a cleaning service.

> When they are interviewed for the fellowship programs, students are told there is an expectation that those selected will give back to the college community in some way. Although the choice of what to do is left up to them, we give them examples of the ways students have fulfilled this expectation in the past. One student, for example set up a display about the Netherlands as part of the new student orientation program. Another wrote an article about her fellowship for her hometown newspaper. And one gave a presentation to allied health classes about Chinese medicine. Even though the contribution students make is not a requirement for the grade, we find on the whole that participants are enthusiastic and more than willing to contribute to the college community in a meaningful way [Clements, 1999].

Students are exposed to a world that is totally different from the one they have known, and they return with a new appreciation for cultural diversity. Through their enthusiasm in class presentations and discussions, along with pictures that are permanently displayed for each fellowship group, they have opened the eyes of all Middlesex students to the value of cultural differences.

5. *Create an international club on campus.* We wanted to encourage collaboration among various ethnic groups of students, and rather than creating a separate club for each ethnic group, the students and staff decided to create one overall club, called the International Club, which would represent all groups. Club participants include those from many different cultures and countries, as well as various racial groups. This club plans celebrations, musical events, lectures, and countless other activities.

6. *Integrate the appreciation of cultural differences into the Freshman Seminar curriculum.* Freshman Seminar is a one-credit course that is team-taught by faculty and student development staff members and is required for all entering students enrolled in the liberal arts and sciences and liberal studies programs. Approximately twenty-five class sections are offered each fall semester and a smaller number are offered in the spring.

We have revised the Freshman Seminar curriculum to include several components that stress the importance of valuing differences. Faculty members who teach in the program can choose from a variety of teaching options, including discussion tapes about diversity issues and exercises that have been developed by staff members. Faculty and staff members who teach Freshman Seminar are trained each year in diversity. In addition, two faculty members and two staff members who teach Freshman Seminar are part of a larger, intense training program that the college has undertaken this year to discuss teaching techniques and to improve the sensitivity of faculty members regarding issues of diversity. The faculty training program for the college this year was possible because of modest grant funding.

These four individuals will revise the Freshman Seminar curriculum even further to include substantive components on diversity issues. The evaluation of these revisions will occur over the next few years.

7. *Develop a student improvisational theater troupe.* Under grant funding that was allocated for one year to Wellesley College, in collaboration with Middlesex and other surrounding colleges, selected Middlesex Community College students and faculty members were able to develop a student improvisational theater troupe that focuses on such pertinent student issues as valuing differences. The grant funding was originally available for only one year, but the troupe has continued for the past several years and appears to be more active each year. The program was initially arranged through the efforts of the director of health services, but it has continued and grown with the collaboration and leadership of a faculty member from the humanities division. When this theater troupe performs, students in the audience really listen, and there is a discussion period after each vignette, during which those in the audience are engaged and responsive. This troupe has received recognition from those beyond the college, and, as time allows, the players perform in public schools and agencies in the surrounding area.

These are the major initiatives that have been developed over the past few years in an effort to create a positive campus climate in which students value differences and appreciate cultural diversity. It is important to emphasize, though, that there have been many initiatives across the whole college community toward this end. Faculty members have received training in Asian and Hispanic cultures, with funding from such organizations as the National Endowment for the Humanities. Faculty members have been actively revising their curricula to reflect appreciation of other cultures. Through the efforts of the dean of economic and community development, the college has had many visitors and scholars from China, Russia, South Africa, Columbia, and countless other countries. Any large-scale effort to change attitudes and create a new campus awareness involves the whole college, and this has been the case at Middlesex Community College.

Impact on Minority Retention

We were eager to know whether these efforts made a difference in student attitudes and whether the minority student retention rate had improved. There are several means of assessment that we use in student development, all of which have been created by the student development staff. First, we distribute a student needs assessment and a separate faculty assessment of student needs every three years; second, we use forms to evaluate our services in every department; third, the dean of student development meets with a faculty focus group, consisting of approximately twenty-five faculty members, as well as a separate student focus group, consisting of thirty students who have been nominated by faculty members; finally, the student development staff has created an outcomes assessment that measures twenty-two areas of affective growth and has been given to graduates for the last several years. The institutional research office provides us with information on retention rates.

We were extremely pleased with the assessment results. In our outcomes assessment, graduating students were asked to measure the influence the college has had on their affective growth, using a four-point Likert scale. One of the statements is, "Becoming aware of people who are different from me in their philosophies, cultures, religions or ways of life." For the 1993 class, graduates placed that statement within the top six of the twenty-two statements that measured the influence the college had had on their growth. In 1996, that statement was listed as the fourth-highest response from graduates. By their response to that statement, more than half the graduates from both classes indicated that the college had "very much influenced" (the highest level on the Likert scale) their growth in this area.

Another response that was listed by graduates within the top five statements that measured the influence the college has had on their affective growth was "Improving my ability to listen and understand what others are saying." Again, more than half the graduates (64 percent) indicated that the college had "very much" influenced their growth in this area. "Our students are clearly more connected with students of other races and cultures, and there is a climate on campus of acceptance and affirmation" (Clements, 1999).

In the students' needs assessment, which was distributed with 543 completed surveys that were representative of the student population, we asked students a variety of questions about the social climate on campus. Students perceived that the racial climate was accepting. Eighty-two percent of the students responded positively to the statement "Students of different races and cultures can feel comfortable and accepted at Middlesex." More than half (56 percent) said that they had made friends with students from different races and cultures while at Middlesex. This was particularly gratifying to us because we hoped that students would move beyond acknowledging other races and cultures on campus, and would actually develop connections with those who were different from themselves. These student connections among difference races and cultures appeared to be happening. However, only 41 percent of the students responded positively to the statement "Students who are gay or lesbian can feel comfortable and accepted at Middlesex." Clearly, the acceptance of gays and lesbians on campus is an area toward which we need to direct more effort.

The written responses from students on the outcomes assessment, and the statements students have given when they met in focus group meetings with the dean speak to the impact they have felt about valuing differences on campus. When students were asked on the outcomes assessment how the college has most influenced them, comments have included "I have developed a respect for every human being," "I have learned to take others into consideration," "I have grown mostly in my relations with other ethnic people, and I enjoy it," "I have become a mature, intelligent woman. I experience others' values, beliefs, and validate them without judgment, in conjunction with finding myself and my place in this world," "I have grown in being independent and self-supportive. I have become more in tune to people's backgrounds and different ways of life. I also have a lot more respect for people of different races," "I have found myself to be more open to others' opinions, ideas. Although I have always been active in anti-racism, I found that I am more sensitive to this and more receptive to people's feelings." Comments from students in the focus group sessions are similar.

In terms of minority student retention, the retention rate for entering minority students from Fall 1988 to Fall 1989 was 40 percent. The Fall 1988 minority group retention was 9 points lower than the overall student retention rate; the Fall 1993 group was only 5 points behind, so there had been some very positive improvement. The retention rate for minority students for Fall 1995 to Fall 1996 was 52 percent, so there has been dramatic improvement. And that improvement has remained relatively steady: minority students were 6 points behind the overall student retention rate from Fall 1997 to Fall 1998.

Minority student retention is based on myriad factors, and it is difficult to know whether the initiatives we have undertaken, which have been campuswide, have had a significant impact on the retention rate of minorities. We can see through the needs assessment, however, that minority students have felt accepted on campus, and that other students have made friends with students from different races and cultures. Campus climate certainly has an impact on the comfort level, and in turn, the retention rate of minority students.

Most of all, we were delighted with the responses our graduates related in the outcomes assessments and the student focus groups. Our students are connected with students of other races and cultures, and there is a climate on campus of acceptance and affirmation. This is exactly what we wanted to achieve. Nevertheless, we are aware that this is a constant effort, and we will continually strive to create new programs and initiatives that encourage our students to understand and appreciate the importance of valuing differences in others.

Reference

Clements, E. "Creating a Campus Climate That Truly Values Diversity." *About Campus*, Nov.–Dec. 1999, pp. 23–25.

EVELYN CLEMENTS is dean of student development at Middlesex Community College in Massachusetts.

The use of educational technology not only facilitates learning but also provides educational access to students at a distance. This chapter outlines issues instructors should consider when integrating technology into the curriculum.

Using Technology to Facilitate Learning for Minority Students

Nilda Palma-Rivas

It is well known that two major influences are currently affecting U.S. society: an increase in the diversity of its population and extremely rapid technological developments. These two powerful influences have become catalysts for change in educational institutions, driving the implementation of new interventions, particularly at community colleges. Implications of these two influences are enormous for the instructional design process and subsequent transfer of knowledge. Consequently, as these two influences constantly evolve, community college instructors face challenges never before experienced.

Student diversity and technology have rarely been treated in conjunction with each other in the education literature. Although much has been written about these two forces separately, not many writers on education have attempted to put them together (Damarin, 1998). Minority student issues and technology education have been pursued independently from each other (Damarin). "Issues such as how technology fits into a conceptual framework of principles for how people learn or into a broader philosophy of teaching and learning are seldom raised" (Grasha and Yangarber-Hicks, 2000, p. 3). Matters of cultural, racial, and ethnic diversity are almost absent in the educational technology literature (Powell, 1997a). Also, questions about the sociocultural implications of software are neglected (Agalianos and Cope, 1994). Therefore, research is now needed to determine the effects of each of these forces on teaching and learning processes.

The purpose of this chapter is to make suggestions in the interest of minority student retention through the use of technologies for learning. The first part of this chapter provides a general background by discussing this country's increasing ethnic diversity and the growth of technological innovations and their relationship to community colleges, as well as technological barriers and the potential benefits of technology to minority students. The second part of this chapter presents suggestions for the effective use of technology with minority students, with a discussion of the importance of (1) having culturally sensitive instructors and (2) successfully adapting instructional design. Suggestions drawn from learning styles theory and pedagogy are incorporated into some instructional design phases, including tips for instructors who work with minority students and technology. This chapter concludes with a discussion of some challenges instructors may face when trying to adapt technology to enhance minority student learning.

Forces Shaping Education at Community Colleges

Minority students. Community colleges enroll a more ethnically diverse student body than any other higher education sector. It is not surprising, then, that most community college classes include students with different learning styles, ways of thinking and communicating, motivational cues, and ethnic and social backgrounds. Several other factors contribute to the increased diversity at community colleges. Some community colleges are not only undertaking aggressive marketing strategies to attract minority students but are also implementing programs to reduce their attrition. It is expected that implementation of distance education will bring in even more diverse students as community colleges reach more geographically dispersed students. As the community college reaches an even greater variety of minority students, the challenge to provide them with the opportunity to succeed in this technological era is even more apparent.

Having a diversity of students brings challenges and concerns. For example, minority students' level of achievement differs from that of their white counterparts, in that black, Latino, and American Indian students generally do not perform as well as white students (Weissert, 1999). Minority students' attrition rates are also much higher than those of their white counterparts. Although many variables hinder the educational progress of minority students, the learning environment in which a student is immersed plays a very important role. If the learning environment does not support their learning patterns, minority students are forced to make difficult and constant adjustments (Guild, 1994). The question for instructors is how to use technology to address these challenges and to diminish these concerns.

Technological developments. Technology is considered one of the major causes of increased work productivity (Green and Gilbert, 1995). To continue to reap the economic benefits of technology, society expects not only computer literate graduates but also graduates with the necessary computer, communication, and information knowledge and skills to be able to work effectively. Therefore, it is not surprising that the application of advanced technology is becoming not only more apparent but also justified in community college environments. For most students, access to information and computers has become one of their first priorities. In an effort to incorporate computer-based technology, many community colleges are changing their curricula and relations with business and industry in the surrounding community. College authorities are making efforts to make available technological resources and programs for instructors and students so that colleges can respond to societal expectations. Commitment to technology is exemplified by making policies flexible, partnering with high-technology companies, investing in hardware and software, changing organizational structures, conducting faculty development, planning strategically, and integrating technology into curricula. As a result, several community colleges are enjoying the reputation of being at the cutting edge of technology. Yet the question remains, are these new technologies assisting or hindering minority students' learning processes?

Technology and Minority Students

Inequity issues. Emerging technologies are cited as vehicles for overcoming inequities. Distance education approaches like interactive television, telecommunications networks, teleconferencing, and the Internet are promoted as avenues for improving resources for minority students (Bruder, 1989). However, despite the promises of emerging technologies, minority students continue to be at a disadvantage. For example, research has shown that black, Latino, and Native American students are less likely than white students to have computer and Internet access in their homes. A study reports that nearly 41 percent of white households own a personal computer, compared with 19.3 percent of black households and 19.4 percent of Hispanic households (Roach, 1998). Therefore, minority students are likely to be among those who do not have technological experience. Students who have access to technology in their homes usually come to the classroom with more highly developed skills and a level of understanding that makes them less dependent on their instructors (Jameson, 1999). Students in poor communities usually do not have such access and therefore depend on getting computer and Internet access at their educational institutions (Roach, 1998) or at other public institutions. Consequently, students with little or no extracurricular experience with technology generally fall behind in or are excluded from activities that require the use of it.

Potential benefits. A wide range of technologies can be used to promote learning. In this chapter, I focus on some of the potential benefits for minority students that computers and network connections provide. Computers are ideal devices to implement principles of interactive learning, to upgrade the level of instruction, and to develop students' abilities for self-learning (Hefzallah, 1990). Computers also provide a high degree of user control.

Computer software, when incorporated thoughtfully into instruction, has the potential to increase the efficiency of the learning experience for minority students in several ways.

First, computer technologies have the potential to change classroom power dynamics. Online communication encourages students to contact their instructor more often than they would in the traditional classroom (Chizmar and Williams, 1996). Electronic mail allows students who are hesitant to become involved in class discussion, such as many minority students are, to communicate privately with instructors rather than having to speak up in class (Gilbert, 1996).

Second, computer technologies allow students to participate in simulated real-life experiences. CD-ROMs and the Internet can offer multimedia case simulations that provide students with the possibility of discussing real-life examples, while giving them the flexibility to incorporate their own viewpoints without any risk. Multimedia case studies can provide peer-based collaborative interaction that gives students the opportunity to learn from one another through the exchange of opinions.

Third, computer-based learning gives students more control over their own learning (Needham, 1986). By working with content posted on the Internet, students can work from anywhere and at their own pace, starting the learning process when they are motivated and stopping when they lose interest (Needham, 1986).

Fourth, Internet-based communication applications such as Webboard encourage active learning and participation. Webboard is essentially a text-based computer conferencing system with multimedia capabilities that can be used both synchronously and asynchronously for the exchange of information between instructors, peers, and subject matter experts. Webboard versatility allows students to work both individually and in groups, thus accommodating several learning styles.

Finally, some Internet-based technologies can satisfy different learning styles by combining different forms of delivery. Technologies such as RealPlayer allow the transmission of text, graphics, photographs, slides, and motion videos and audio. This significantly expands curricula. More sophisticated programs such as expert systems encourage students to develop critical thinking and problem-solving skills (Furger, 1999).

Suggestions for the Effective Use of Technology with Minority Students

Culturally sensitive instructors. The first requirement for effective use of technology with minority students is to have culturally sensitive instructors and designers. In the broader sense, "culturally sensitive" means understanding and accepting other cultures. A culturally sensitive instructor "creates learning experiences and environments with the realization that each learner has distinctive communication and learning styles, orientation and value system [s that are] culturally based and influenced" (Powell, 1997b, p. 6). Therefore, culturally sensitive instructors are able not only to recognize that minority students bring with them a variety of talents, learning styles, motivational cues, and cognitive orientations but also to create and evaluate instructional strategies that can incorporate these diverse needs. If instructors are not sensitive to cultural issues, they are not going to understand that it is necessary to accommodate people from different backgrounds. If they have not developed cultural sensitivity, they are not going to understand how technology can hinder minority students' learning, and they may not be aware of what to do to make technology work for minority students.

Instructors and instructional designers can increase their level of cultural sensitivity by reflecting on their practices. Powell (1997b) proposes a guide that can help instructors work more effectively. He suggests identifying what form of educational system is most familiar to students, how students perceive instructors, what kind of learning environment is most suitable for students, what kind of intelligent assessment instruments are fair and unbiased, what kind of relationship is most natural for students, what type of reward is appealing to students, what mode of discipline is most effective, and what the students' cognitive styles and attitudes are toward achievement. Considering all these variables is critical because it makes instruction sensitive to differences, which is more important than the technology itself. Instructors must not forget that the success or failure of technology depends largely on its implementation.

Planning using instructional design. It is important for instructors to remember that the use of technology does not ensure quality of instruction (Florini, 1990). Choosing a piece of technology just because it looks promising or because it has proved to have benefits somewhere else is not a sound pedagogical decision. By doing that, instructors run the risk of misapplying technologies and hindering the learning process instead of assisting it. Careful planning is one step toward ensuring meaningful learning, in that it will help instructors not only to take advantage of the potential benefits of technology but also to determine its potential disadvantages. Without comprehensive planning, education will continue to fall short of preparing minority students. Therefore, it is important for instructors who want to incorporate technology into their courses to carefully plan what technologies they are going to use and how they might affect minority students' learning. Instructors should also ask themselves why they would like to use a specific technology. One way to approach these decisions is through the use of instructional design.

Instructional design (ID) is a systematic development of instruction that leads to the arrangement of events, content, learning materials, and experiences to achieve goals. It focuses on the learner to produce meaningful learning. Sometimes technology does not bring the expected outcomes. The failure of technology has been associated with the incompatibility between the technology and the instructional design process. Consequently, to reap the potential benefits that technology offers to minority students, it is necessary to conduct a deliberate, thorough, and careful ID process. When working with a diverse student body and trying to incorporate technology into the learning process, it may be necessary to pay special attention to certain steps of the instructional design process. Analyzing learners' characteristics, developing instructional strategies, and developing and selecting instructional materials are steps of the ID process that instructors must not disregard.

Analyzing learners' characteristics: integrating technology and minority students' learning styles. A very critical step in the ID process is learner analysis, especially if the student body is very diverse. By conducting a learner analysis through a survey, for instance, instructors can create learning environments that support differences. The results of the learner analysis will show who students are and what instructional strategies, materials, and technologies are most appropriate for them. Specifically, this step will allow the instructor to discover minority students' needs, their learning styles, their motivational cues, and so forth. Taking into account students' learning styles has proved to have positive results (Dunn, Beaudry, and Klavas, 1989). The challenge instructors face is how to make technology compatible with the learning styles of minority students.

Studies in the field of learning styles support the fact that people from different cultures present very distinctive ways of learning. In linking learning styles with culture, Hilliard (1992) found that African Americans share similar learning style patterns. Based on the fact that African Americans value oral experiences and interpersonal relationships, Guild (1994) suggests that classroom activities for them should include discussion, active projects, and collaborative assignments. Another study examining learning styles among Hispanics found a similar phenomenon. Hispanics prefer cognitive generalizations and personal relationship activities (Vasquez and others, 1999). More (1990) and Aragon, Sanchez, and Boverie (2000) also found similar learning styles among Native Americans. More found that Native Americans require quiet times for thinking and prefer visual stimuli to other sensory stimuli. Aragon, Sanchez, and Boverie found that Native Americans and Hispanics have similar learning preferences, with some exceptions. Although minority groups do share similar learning styles, it is important not to generalize too much because, within groups, variations exist as well. Boutte and DeFlorimonte (1998) advise coupling cultural differences with information about each student, because each person is a unique cultural entity.

There have been some efforts to match technologies with some learning styles. Tomei (1997) proposed an analysis by matching technology with a student's level of autonomy. He concludes that computer conferencing, the Internet, computer-based training, videoconferencing, and e-mail require high levels of autonomy on the student's part. On the other hand, computer-delivered instruction and computer-managed instruction require student dependency on instructors. Students with limited autonomy can use audio conferences, video only, and audio only.

Ross and Schulz (1999) explain how to adapt the Internet to learning styles. Specifically, they describe how it can be used for visual, auditory, and hands-on learning styles. For students who learn best through sight, instructors can provide animation, compressed video clips, animated information, online overhead presentations, and even virtual reality exercises. For students whose best way of learning is by listening, instructors can record their lectures and publish them over the Internet, where other students can listen to or download them. For students who learn best by doing or putting into practice, instructors should provide problem-solving exercises, hands-on activities, brainstorming ideas, case studies, and simulations. Ross and Schulz discuss the social aspects of the Internet, where collaborative people can benefit from interacting with others, including peers, instructors, and even subject matter experts. Listservs, e-mails, chat rooms, Internet-based pagers, and bulletin boards are good sources for discussion.

Undoubtedly, trying to put together technologies, learning styles, and culture makes the teaching process extremely complex. However, instructors should keep in mind that "using technology alone without considering individual differences articulated by learning styles is futile" (James and Gardner, 1995, p. 27). Consequently, once the instructors have identified their students' learning styles and preferences, the best way of approaching technology and learning differences is by including them when developing instructional strategies.

Developing instructional strategies by integrating technology with minority students' learning styles. At this stage, instructors organize content so that students can process it cognitively. The organization the instructor gives to content may not necessarily match the way minority students process information. Therefore, instructors should make an effort to organize and present content in different ways. Ross and Schulz (1999) match Internet-based activities with cognitive processes (Gregorc, 1982). A concrete sequential learner is one who learns best by having sequential information and prefers activities that are based on task analysis, flowcharts, and cause-effect relationships. They can benefit from such applications as online virtual labs, posting solutions to problems, and PowerPoint lectures. Concrete random students are those who learn best by processing tangible information, and they prefer activities that are based on exploration, problem solving, and hypothetical thinking. They learn best from case studies, independent study ideas, and linking to previous work published on the Internet. Abstract sequential learners are people who learn best through activities that involve reason and intuition. They prefer such activities as interpretation, abstraction, and logical analysis, and they benefit from Internet-based applications that make reference to further studies and online study resources. Abstract random learners are students who learn best by using multidimensional thinking and enjoy activities that have some degree of analysis, creativity, and mind mapping. They benefit from Internet-based applications that incorporate links, chat rooms, newsgroups, bulletin boards, and course discussions through listservs.

Developing instructional strategies is a key step in satisfying minority students' learning styles. In this phase of instructional design, instructors should ensure that they incorporate a variety of activities to reach a wide spectrum of learning styles. Instructors must then design their instruction with learner differences in mind. For example, instructors could present content through as many choices as possible. New technologies allow text to be presented in different colors, sounds, photos, full-motion video, and graphics that can make instruction very engaging. This gives students the opportunity and flexibility to choose the modality that best fits their learning style. A hybrid delivery mode that mixes face-to-face instruction with online instruction by using Internet technologies can provide the widest range of content delivery to promote effective learning. By using the Internet, instructors can deliver their information in different ways, such as by audio or visual means, or by having their students learn by doing, through involvement in, for example, a case study. People from underrepresented cultures generally prefer active participation as a way of learning. The Internet also allows social participation modes and can satisfy a wide variety of cognitive styles.

Through the use of the Internet, instructors have the opportunity to create instructional strategies that can lead to individualized instruction as well. For students who are not competitive, computers can provide self-paced, noncompetitive, and nonthreatening activities. Some minority students need more time because of their learning styles, language barriers, and accessibility issues; therefore, instructors should also think of self-paced activities. Students can access self-paced activities posted on the Internet from anywhere at any time. However, when assigning self-paced, technology-based activities, instructors should keep in mind the issues of accessibility and inequity.

Instructors should provide a supportive environment that motivates minority students to learn the content and to use the technology involved. One way of creating a supportive environment is by including students' experiences and media preferences in the learning strategy. Another way of doing it is by using technologies available through the Internet. Internet-based pagers, e-mail, listservs, and newsgroups allow the exchange of information at extremely high speeds. Instructors should also plan instructional strategies that satisfy group as well as individual learning.

Developing and selecting materials: integrating technology and minority students. Instructors should not forget that materials must be aligned with goals and objectives for them to be effective. Instructors should therefore analyze their goals first and then determine which technology can be useful in achieving them. The main objective then is to enhance minority students' learning and not merely the use of technology. There are two options: to develop or to select the needed materials. When developing materials to be delivered through the use of certain technologies, instructors should make sure that the material is not biased and that the language usage is appropriate and inoffensive. This is difficult because every person has intrinsic biases that he or she may not even be aware of. Therefore, materials should be pilot-tested by people from different ethnic groups and changes should be made according to their feedback. This is one way of minimizing the risk of hindering minority students' learning.

Selecting appropriate instructional materials for students is challenging because the individuals in a given classroom can be a confounding mix of ages, ability levels, interests, and cultural experiences (Hilgendorf, 1998). Even though computers and technology have been regarded as "neutral" tools, they may not be adequate or may even become negative for certain ethnic groups. Research has shown that some software may be rated very low in this respect. Agalianos and Cope (1994) focused their analysis on educational programs used for simulations and found that this type of software may reinforce ethnic imbalances through character description and depicted action, may show little sensitivity to multicultural issues, and may be biased with regard to roles. Bigelow (1997) found a CD-ROM program to be culturally insensitive and racist. The rationale provided by these researchers is that it is generally people from the dominant culture who develop software. Therefore, a sound pedagogical decision is to question and analyze the potential sociocultural implications of computer-based programs. DeVillar and Faltis (1991) state that because of the limitations of software, instructors should analyze the pedagogical soundness of computer programs prior to and during the time students are using it. Miller-Lachman (1994) recommends that instructors assess software by observing how minorities are portrayed, the attention their respective cultures receive, the accuracy of their representation, the language used, how distorted illustrations may be, the emphasis placed on minority characters, and the roles performed by minorities. One way to approach this issue is by creating committees composed of people from different backgrounds who will examine and evaluate the technology to be used.

Conclusion

Trying to find a point where technology and minority students' characteristics meet to produce meaningful learning is a very difficult task for any instructor. Accommodating students from different backgrounds may become more difficult when trying to find the right technology for them. To begin with, trying to be a reflective instructor who constantly analyzes his or her assumptions and biases is complex because not everyone knows whether his or her assumptions are right or not. It can become a tiring and burdensome process. In addition, finding the right balance between the learning styles of different groups and individuals is challenging and time-consuming. Finally, when creating instructional strategies and developing and selecting materials, many variables must be taken into consideration. However, instructors should attempt to address all of these complexities in order to make instruction more responsive to the diverse backgrounds of their students. It is hoped that in the near future there will not only be more technology and software based on different learning styles and cultural experiences but that there will also be research that can better guide the instructor. In the meantime, these strategies can be employed to help bring about the successful use of technology to accommodate the different learning styles of minority students.

References

Agalianos, A., and Cope, P. "Information Technology and Knowledge: The Non-Neutrality of Content-Specific Educational Software." *Journal of Education Policy*, 1994, *9*(1), 35–45.

Aragon, S., Sanchez, I., and Boverie, P. "A Comparative Analysis of Postsecondary American Indian and Hispanic Student Learning Styles." Paper presented at the American Educational Research Association Annual Meeting, New Orleans, Apr. 24–28, 2000.

Bigelow, B. "On the Road to Cultural Bias: A Critique of 'The Oregon Trail' CD-ROM." *Language Arts*, 1997, *74*(2), 84–93.

Boutte, G. S., and DeFlorimonte, D. "The Complexities of Valuing Cultural Differences Without Overemphasizing Them: Taking It to the Next Level." *Equity and Excellence in Education*, 1998, *31*(3), 54–62.

Bruder, I. "Distance Learning: What's Holding Back This Boundless System?" *Electronic Learning*, 1989, *8*(6), 30–35.

Chizmar, J. F., and Williams, D. "Altering Time and Space Through Network Technologies to Enhance Learning." *Cause/Effect*, 1996, *19*(3), 14–21.

Damarin, K. S. "Technology and Multicultural Education: The Question of Convergence." *Theory into Practice*, 1998, *37*(1), 11–19.

DeVillar, R., and Faltis, C. *Computers and Cultural Diversity: Restructuring for School Success*. Albany, N.Y.: State University of New York Press, 1991.

Dunn, R., Beaudry, J., and Klavas, A. "Survey of Research on Learning Styles." *Educational Leadership*, 1989, *46*(6), 50–58.

Florini, B. "Communication Technologies in Adult Education." In M. W. Galbraith (ed.), *Adult Learning Methods*. Malabar, Fla.: Krieger, 1990.

Furger, R. "Are Wired Schools Failing Our Kids?" *PC World*, 1999, *17*(9), 148–152.

Gilbert, S. "Making the Most of a Slow Revolution." *Change*, 1996, *28*(2), 10–23.

Grasha, A., and Yangarber-Hicks, N. "Integrating Teaching Styles and Learning Styles with Instructional Technologies." *College Teaching*, 2000, *48*(1), 2–10.

Gregorc, A. "Learning/Teaching Styles: Potent Forces Behind Them." *Educational Leadership*, 1982, *36*(4), 234–236.

Green, K., and Gilbert, S. "Great Expectations." *Change*, 1995, *27*(2), 8–18.

Guild, P. "The Culture/Learning Style Connection." *Educational Leadership*, 1994, *51*(8), 16–21.

Hefzallah, I. *The New Learning and Telecommunications Technologies: Their Potential Applications in Education*. Springfield, Ill.: Thomas, 1990.

Hilgendorf, T. "CD-ROM Technology for Developing College-Level Skills." *Journal of Adolescent and Adult Literacy*, 1998, *41*(6), 475.

Hilliard, A. G. "Behavioral Style, Culture, and Teaching and Learning." *Journal of Negro Education*, 1992, *61*(3), 370–377.

James, W., and Gardner, D. "Learning Styles: Implications for Distance Learning." In M. H. Rossman and M. E. Rossman (eds.), *Facilitating Distance Education.* New Directions for Adult and Continuing Education, no. 67. San Francisco: Jossey-Bass, 1995.

Jameson, R. "Equity and Access to Educational Technology." *Thrust for Educational Leadership,* 1999, *28*(4), 28–31.

Miller-Lachman, L. "Bytes & Bias: Eliminating Cultural Stereotypes from Educational Software." *School Library Journal,* 1994, *40*(11), 26–30.

More, A. J. *Learning Styles of Native Americans and Asians.* Paper presented at the 98th Annual Meeting of the American Psychological Association, Boston, Mass., Aug. 13, 1990. (ED 330 535)

Needham, R. *Are Communications Technologies in Education a Threat to Faculty?* ERIC Digest, 1986. (ED 269 114)

Powell, G. "Diversity and Educational Technology: Introduction to Special Issue." *Educational Technology,* 1997a, *37*(2), 5.

Powell, G. "On Being a Culturally Sensitive Instructional Designer and Educator." *Educational Technology,* 1997b, *37*(2), 6–14.

Roach, R. "The Networking Imperative." *Black Issues in Higher Education,* 1998, *15*(13), 30–32.

Ross, J., and Schulz, R. "Using the World Wide Web to Accommodate Diverse Learning Styles." *College Teaching,* 1999, *47*(4), 123–129.

Tomei, L. "Instructional Technology: Pedagogy for the Future." *T.H.E. Journal,* 1997, *25*(12), 56–59.

Vasquez, G., and others. *Computer-Based Technology and Learning: Evolving Uses and Expectations.* Oak Brook, Ill.: NCREL, 1999.

Weissert, W. "Report Cites Gap in Student Performance." *Chronicle of Higher Education,* 1999, *46*(10), A42.

NILDA PALMA-RIVAS is an educational technology consultant and former administrator of HRE Online at the University of Illinois, Urbana-Champaign.

8

For white faculty members to be effective in a minority institution, they must be aware of how their racial identity affects their perceptions, content knowledge, and classroom values, and they must be willing to share these insights with their students.

Integrating Nonminority Instructors into the Minority Environment

Barbara K. Townsend

In 1996–97, more than 90 two-year colleges had a student body that was predominantly black, Hispanic, or Native American. These institutions included 14 two-year historically black colleges, 26 predominantly black colleges, 21 predominantly Hispanic, and 29 tribal colleges (Townsend, 1999). In addition, during that same academic year, over 50 two-year institutions had a student body that was predominantly minority. For example, in 1996–97, 83 percent of Miami-Dade Community College's fifty-one thousand plus students were minorities: 59 percent Hispanic, 22 percent black, and 2 percent Asian or Pacific Islander (*Peterson's Guide,* 1997).

Although over half the students at these colleges are nonwhite, many of their instructors are white. Over 25 percent of the faculty at two-year historically black colleges are white (Foster, Guyden, and Miller, 1999), and almost two-thirds of tribal college faculty members are white (Boyer, 1997, p. 32). At only 5 two-year colleges do black instructors constitute more than 50 percent of the faculty. Similarly, Hispanic instructors make up over 25 percent of the faculty at only 3 two-year colleges, and at no colleges are they in the majority. When Hispanic and black faculty members are combined, they become the majority of instructors at only 2 two-year colleges ("Fifty Top Colleges by Number of Black Faculty," 2000).

Thus, white faculty members are in the majority at most community colleges, including those at which over half the students are nonwhite. What is it like to be a white or nonminority faculty member at a minority institution? How does this situation differ from being a minority faculty member at a predominantly white college? In this chapter I compare the experiences of minority faculty members at majority institutions with those of nonminority faculty members at colleges where the student enrollment is predominantly minority. I also provide some recommendations on how a nonminority faculty member can be an effective teacher at a minority institution.

Faculty Members as Racial/Ethnic Minorities at Their Institution

In an ideal world, being a faculty member whose racial or ethnic group is different from that of most people at a college or university would not matter. However, in the real world, being "different" because of one's race or ethnicity may affect one's relationships with students as well as with fellow faculty members. Certainly, the literature is replete with stories and studies of the difficulties minority faculty and staff members encounter at predominantly white colleges and universities (for example, de la Luz Reyes and Halcon, 1988/1996; Gregory, 1995; Harvey, 1999; Olsen, Maple, and Stage, 1995; Rains, 1998, Stein, 1996).

Mitchell (1983/1998) describes minority faculty members as being "visible, vulnerable, and viable" (p. 257). Most minority faculty members have high physical visibility at a majority institution. They are also very "vulnerable" to demands not only from their academic community but also from their racial/ethnic community. For Native Americans, "the social value and preeminent goal in life . . . is the survival of the Indian people" (Cross, 1996, p. 335), and Native American faculty members share this goal (Stein, 1996). Similarly, Chicano faculty members typically "maintain a strong affiliation with their community and feel a strong sense of responsibility to improve the status of other Chicanos in the larger community" (de la Luz Reyes and Halcon, 1988/1996, p. 345; see also Rendon, 1992/1996). For African American faculty members, ties with the black community are usually very important, partly because of "the African heritage of communalism" (Gregory, 1995, p. 7). Balancing commitments to one's racial or ethnic community with commitments to one's institution and the broader academic community is difficult partly because of the time required to meet both communities' demands. The demands may also be "philosophically and culturally disparate in their orientation" (Mitchell, 1983/1998, p. 262), rendering "[m]inority faculty members whose area of specialization involves ethnic communities . . . particularly vulnerable to conflicts between the criteria of the university and the community" (p. 260). The university community's demands for objective research, couched in the language of the discipline, conflict with a minority community's desire for "research that advocates change, that helps to get money, and that speaks in plain language" (p. 260). To succeed as minority faculty members in a predominantly white institution, these instructors must develop a bicultural awareness of the norms of both their racial/ethnic community and their professional community, and they must "situate themselves in the overlap between the two" (p. 262).

Although fairly "visible," nonminority faculty members at a minority institution are not vulnerable to the same extent that minority faculty members are at a majority institution because most whites do not consciously think of themselves as white and therefore having a racial community to which they must contribute to improve its status (McIntosh, 1988/1995; McIntyre, 1997). The few works that have focused on the experiences of nonminority faculty members at a minority institution, however, suggest that in such situations, nonminority faculty members do become aware of their own racial identity, usually for the first time in their lives. Henzy's remarks (1999) are typical of this insight: "[A]s I walked into my first classes that September (at an historically black college), for the first time in my life I felt really white. I had always thought of myself generically as just a person. Now I was conscious of myself specifically as a white person" (p. 17). Similarly, Bales (1999) wrote about being outside a classroom during his first week at the historically black Xavier University and realizing, "[M]ine was the only white face in sight. I was immersed for a brief moment in a scene where I was the different one" (p. 38).

Many nonwhite faculty members working at a minority institution may experience racial discrimination for the first time. In an edited book about the experiences of nonwhite faculty members teaching at historically black colleges and universities (Foster, Guyden, and Miller, 1999), some faculty members wrote about what they perceived to be racism directed toward white faculty. At a two-year historically black college (HBC), a white colleague of mine claimed that "some of the black leadership in the college did not believe that a white person was capable of understanding the depths of what it meant to be black in America and, therefore, [were] not capable of making certain decisions" (Sides-Gonzales, 1999, p. 177). At another four-year HBC, the president announced in a faculty meeting that she held white faculty members to higher expectations than the nonwhite faculty members. Why? Because the white faculty members' "ancestors had established conditions that kept her ancestors suppressed" (Redinger, 1999, p. 33).

Being in the minority, whether because of one's racial or ethnic group or gender, or for any other reason, is typically not a comfortable situation. It may be particularly difficult for people who are used to being in the majority. Becoming aware that they too have a racial identity and learning what it is like to be a minority in a particular setting helps nonminority faculty members develop an increased "sensitivity to issues of minority participation and inclusion" (Thomson, 1999, p. 60).

Part of this sensitivity includes understanding that, unlike minority instructors in a majority institution, white faculty members, because of their race, are in a position of power and privilege within society. Although they may experience racial discrimination directed against them while teaching in a minority college, white faculty members can "on a daily basis . . . escape that experience and reenter a familiar world" (Redinger, 1999, p. 34) in which they are the powerful majority. Perhaps in gaining this understanding, nonminority faculty members have achieved a kind of bicultural awareness that helps them be more professionally "viable" in the context of the minority institution. However, developing viability within the larger professional community of one's academic discipline does not have a racial or ethnic dimension to it for nonminority faculty members. Unlike minority faculty members, nonminority faculty members are generally not criticized, at least by most academics, for doing work that focuses on their own racial group. Mitchell (1983/1998) makes this point when she states how minority faculty members conducting research on their own community run the risk of having this research viewed as having "a self-referential level that the work of nonminority faculty members seems not to possess" (p. 260).

Being an Effective Faculty Member at a Minority College

What are some recommendations for being an effective nonminority faculty member at a minority institution? Because being an effective teacher may be the area of most concern for nonminority faculty members, it seems logical to begin with recommendations on effective teaching.

A well-known article about what constitutes good teaching is Chickering and Gamson's "Seven Principles for Good Practice in Undergraduate Education" (1987/1997). Chickering and Gamson's principles can be construed as recommendations for effective teaching. If written as recommendations, they might read as follows:

- Have contact with your students both in and outside the classroom.
- Develop reciprocity and cooperation among students.
- Use active learning techniques.
- Give prompt feedback.
- Emphasize time on tasks.
- Communicate high expectations.
- Respect diverse talents and ways of learning.

These recommendations seem like common sense to me, but I am a white, middle-class person born in the United States. A brief look at cultures of classrooms in other countries reveals that some of these recommendations are culture-bound. For example, the recommendation to use active learning techniques in which students work with others to learn would not be an effective one at universities in many Asian countries, in which faculty members, rather than students, are viewed as the authority in the classroom (George, 1995). In such a context, the professor or instructor as "sage on the stage" is expected, whereas the professor or instructor as "guide by the side" would be discomforting for many Asian students. Another example is the principle of emphasizing time on task. Even within the United States, this principle is culture-bound. According to Watson and

Terrell (1999), Hispanic Americans like the "freedom to move about and take breaks" (p. 50) and some African Americans "may respond poorly to timed, scheduled, preplanned activities that interfere with immediacy of response" (p. 49). If a faculty member considers time on task to mean sustained, concentrated effort within a limited time frame, this expectation may cause tension between her and some students.

It is interesting to note that Chickering and Gamson's explanation of the principle "Respects diverse talents and ways of learning" (1987/1997, p. 546) does not include any references to diversity stemming from one's race or ethnicity. Rather, the authors see styles of learning in terms of preferences for hands-on experience versus theory, or for setting one's own pace in learning.

Another perspective on effective teaching is found in Grieve's (1996) handbook of advice to adjunct and part-time faculty. Grieve states that "good teaching" means the following (p. 3):

- Knowing your subject content
- Knowing and liking your students
- Understanding our culture
- Possessing command of professional teaching skills and strategies

For those unsure of what Grieve means by "our culture," the only explanation given is, "Understanding our culture has become more complex for today's instructor. Sensitivity to the diverse cultures in your classroom is necessary to success in teaching" (p. 3). Grieve seems to be saying that "our culture" consists of "diverse cultures." This is an important point for all faculty members to understand and remember. They must also understand that their own racial background affects their perspective on the teaching-learning process.

Being professionally viable within a minority college means being trusted and respected by one's colleagues and students. Probably the most important thing nonminority faculty members can do to achieve this viability is to *acknowledge their racial identity and how it frames their perspective and behavior.* For this to happen, nonminority faculty members must first begin to understand that it is not only blacks or Hispanics or Native Americans or Asian/Pacific Islanders who have a racial identity. So, too, do whites. Once white faculty members are conscious of their own racial identity, they can begin to see how it affects their behavior, their knowledge base, and their perceptions of appropriate classroom behavior.

Becoming aware of one's whiteness is a natural by-product of teaching at a minority institution, as has already been indicated. Becoming aware of how being white affects one's interactions with students is more problematic. Whiteness as a racial identity is now a topic of scholarly study (see Delgago and Stefancic, 1997; Frankenberg, 1993), and some attention has been paid to the effect of white K–12 teachers' racial identity on their teaching (see McIntyre, 1997). A few white authors writing about teaching in a minority college or university have indicated how their racial identity influences their teaching. For example, Henzy (1999) believed that as a white, middle-class suburbanite, he automatically or customarily emphasized the importance of abstract thinking—a type of thinking that permeates "America's formal teaching methods and curriculum" (Watson and Terrell, 1999). Cultural differences in how one learns can affect what happens in the classroom because there may be a cultural mismatch between how the faculty member thinks students should learn and how students are used to learning. Thus, nonminority faculty members need to be aware of their cultural or "white" expectations of student learning (Watson and Terrell, 1999; see also George, 1995).

How can white faculty members become aware of their "whiteness" and its implications in the classroom? During the 1980s and 1990s, workshops in diversity training and multicultural education were a popular means of sensitizing white faculty members to cultural diversity in the classroom (see Harris and Kayes, 1995; Harris and Shyrel, 1996). A criticism of this approach is that it typically addresses characteristics that differentiate people—such as race, ethnicity, and gender—but "mute[s] attention to racism (and ignore[s] patriarchy and control by wealth), focusing mainly on cultural difference[s]" (Sleeter, 1994, p. 5).

Less typical efforts to address racial identity include study groups, which are sometimes funded by the institution and are sometimes developed informally among faculty and staff members. For example, when I was a faculty member at Loyola University Chicago, the School of Education Multicultural Committee met regularly in the early 1990s to discuss diversity in the school and the university. It was here that I first became truly conscious of my "whiteness," as we spent sessions discussing our racial identity and its implications for us as individuals. When I moved to the University of Memphis, I participated in a semester-long study group funded by that university. We each received copies of several books designed to increase faculty members' understanding of the intersection of race, class, and gender (see Quadagno, 1994) and met every three to four weeks to discuss them. The conversations were often angry and even hostile, as the racially mixed group discussed the effects of race and gender on social class. As painful and unpleasant as these discussions sometimes were, they forced group members to become more aware of their racial identity and its possible effects upon their social class and attitudes. While at Memphis and now at the University of Missouri-Columbia, I have belonged to informal groups that wanted to discuss current works about race, ethnicity, and gender. These monthly meetings with other women open to discussing their racial identity have helped me to better understand my own.

Self-awareness of one's racial identity and how it informs one's expectations about learning styles and appropriate classroom behavior is vital if a nonminority instructor is to be successful in a minority classroom. It is equally important for faculty members to be honest with students about how an instructor's cultural background affects his or her ability and subject matter expertise. For example, one English instructor, in his first semester at a historically black college, had trouble pronouncing his students' names correctly because he was unused to names that are common among African Americans. Sensing his students' growing impatience and realizing he was about to lose the class, he decided to be open with his students and acknowledge "the limitations of . . . [his white, middle-class, suburban] background" in which people were only named "Billy or Betty or Sally or Tommy." As a result, the students relaxed, and "teaching [was] possible again" (Henzy, 1999, p. 18).

This same faculty member also increased his acceptance among his students by directly addressing what he as a white person could bring to discussions of works by black authors, particularly those who write about their experiences with racial discrimination. Acknowledging to his students that they had a far better cultural understanding of the content of some of these works, he stated that what *he* could contribute was his knowledge of "the abstractions of pattern, symbol, allusion, and theme" (Henzy, 1999, p. 20), a knowledge he had gained not only from formal study but also from his cultural background: "the abstract homogeneity of middle-class suburbia" (p. 21).

Conclusion

Being an effective nonminority faculty member at a minority institution demands a level of awareness about one's self and one's racial identity—and how this racial identity influences one's teaching—that is not the norm for majority faculty members teaching at majority institutions. Therein lies the challenge and the reward. The insight gained about one's teaching will be beneficial in any other academic setting, while the insight gained about how one's race affects one's behavior will benefit relations with people of all races.

References

Bales, F. "Communicating and Learning the Right Message." In L. Foster, J. A. Guyden, and A. L. Miller (eds.), *Affirmed Action: Essays on the Academic and Social Lives of White Faculty Members at Historically Black Colleges and Universities.* New York: Rowman & Littlefield, 1999.

Boyer, P. *Native American Colleges: Progress and Prospects.* San Francisco: Jossey-Bass, 1997.

Chickering, A. W., and Gamson, Z. F. "Seven Principles for Good Practice in Undergraduate Education." In K. Feldman and M. B. Paulsen (eds.), *Teaching and Learning in the College Classroom.* New York: Simon & Schuster Custom Publishing, 1987/1997.

Cross, W. T. "Pathways to the Professoriate: The American Indian Faculty Pipeline." In C. Turner, M. Garcia, A. Nora, and L. I. Rendon (eds.), *Racial and Ethnic Diversity in Higher Education.* New York: Simon & Schuster Custom Publishing, 1988–1996.

de la Luz Reyes, M., and Halcon, J. J. "Racism in Academia: The Old Wolf Revisited." In C. Turner, M. Garcia, A. Nora, and L. I. Rendon (eds.), *Racial and Ethnic Diversity in Higher Education.* New York: Simon & Schuster Custom Publishing, 1988/1996.

Delgago, R., and Stefancic, J. (eds.). *Critical White Studies: Looking Behind the Mirror.* Philadelphia: Temple University Press, 1997.

"Fifty Top Colleges by Number of Black Faculty—Fall 1997." *Community College Week,* 2000, *12*(23) [http://www.ccweek.com/top_99/50top_faculty.html]. Accessed June 28, 2000.

Foster, L., Guyden, J. A., and Miller, A. L. (eds.). *Affirmed Action: Essays on the Academic and Social Lives of White Faculty Members at Historically Black Colleges and Universities.* New York: Rowman & Littlefield, 1999.

Frankenberg, R. *White Women, Race Matters: The Social Construction of Whiteness.* Minneapolis: University of Minnesota Press, 1993.

George, P. G. *College Teaching Abroad: A Handbook of Strategies for Successful Cross-Cultural Exchanges.* Boston: Allyn and Bacon, 1995.

Gregory, S. *Black Women in the Academy: The Secrets to Success and Achievement.* Lanham, Md.: University Press of America, 1995.

Grieve, D. *A Handbook for Adjunct/Part-Time Faculty and Teachers of Adults.* (3rd ed.) Elyria, Ohio: Info-tec, 1996.

Harris, A., and Shyrel, H. "Welcoming Diversity: Celebrating our Differences and Acknowledging our Common Experiences." In *The Olympics of Leadership: Overcoming Obstacles, Balancing Skills, Taking Risks.* Proceedings of the Annual International Conference of the National Community College Chair Academy, Phoeniz, Ariz., 1996. (ED 394 598)

Harris, Z. M., and Kayes, P. "Multicultural and International Challenges to the Community College: A Model for College-Wide Proactive Response." Paper presented at the annual convention of the American Association of Community Colleges, Minneapolis, Minn., 1995.

Harvey, W. R. (ed.). *Grass Roots and Glass Ceilings: African-American Administrators in Predominantly White Colleges and Universities.* Ithaca: State University of New York Frontier Series, 1999.

Henzy, K. "Making Connections: A White Professor at a Historically Black University." In L. Foster, J. A. Guyden, and A. L. Miller (eds.), *Affirmed Action: Essays on the Academic and Social Lives of White Faculty Members at Historically Black Colleges and Universities.* New York: Rowman & Littlefield, 1999.

McIntosh, P. "White Privilege and Male Privilege: A Personal Account of Coming to See Correspondence Through Work in Women's Studies." In M. L. Anderson and P. H. Collins (eds.), *Race, Class, and Gender: An Anthology.* Belmont, Calif.: Wadsworth, 1988/1995.

McIntyre, A. *Making Meaning of Whiteness: Exploring Racial Identity with White Teachers.* Albany, N.Y.: State University of New York Press, 1997.

Mitchell, J. "Visible, Vulnerable, and Viable: Emerging Perspectives of a Minority Professor." In K. Feldman and M. B. Paulsen (eds.), *Teaching and Learning in the College Classroom.* New York: Simon & Schuster Custom Publishing, 1983/1998.

Olsen, D., Maple, S. A., and Stage, F. A. "Women and Minority Faculty Job Satisfaction: Professional Role Interests, Professional Satisfactions, and Institutional Fit." *Journal of Higher Education,* 1995, *66*(3), 267–293.

Peterson's Guide to Two-Year Colleges 1998. Princeton, N.J.: Peterson's Guides, 1997.

Quadagno, J. *The Color of Welfare.* New York: Oxford University Press, 1994.

Rains, F. V. "Dancing on the Sharp Edge of the Sword: Women Faculty of Color in White Academe." In L. K. Christian-Smith and K. S. Kellor (eds.), *Everyday Knowledge and Women of the Academy: Uncommon Truths.* Boulder, Colo.: Westview Press, 1998.

Redinger, M. A. "You Just Wouldn't Understand." In L. Foster, J. A. Guyden, and A. L. Miller (eds.), *Affirmed Action: Essays on the Academic and Social Lives of White Faculty Members at Historically Black Colleges and Universities.* New York: Rowman & Littlefield, 1999.

Rendon, L. "From the Barrio to the Academy: Revelations of a Mexican-American 'Scholarship Girl.' " In C. Turner, M. Garcia, A. Nora, and L. I. Rendon (eds.), *Racial and Ethnic Diversity in Higher Education.* New York: Simon & Schuster Custom Publishing, 1992/1996.

Sides-Gonzales, K. "Educating as Moral Responsibility." In L. Foster, J. A. Guyden, and A. L. Miller (eds.), *Affirmed Action: Essays on the Academic and Social Lives of White Faculty Members at Historically Black Colleges and Universities.* New York: Rowman & Littlefield, 1999.

Sleeter, C. "Multicultural Education, Social Positionality, and Whiteness." Paper presented at the annual meeting of the American Education Research Association, New Orleans, 1994.

Stein, W. "The Survival of American Indian Faculty." In C. Turner, M. Garcia, A. Nora, and L. I. Rendon (eds.), *Racial and Ethnic Diversity in Higher Education.* New York: Simon & Schuster Custom Publishing, 1996.

Thomson, M. A. "The 'Science' and 'Art' of Teaching and Learning at Xavier University of Louisiana." In L. Foster, J. A. Guyden, and A. L. Miller (eds.), *Affirmed Action: Essays on the Academic and Social Lives of White Faculty Members at Historically Black Colleges and Universities.* New York: Rowman & Littlefield, 1999.

Townsend, B. K. "Collective and Distinctive Patterns of Two-Year Special Focus Colleges." In B. Townsend (ed.), *Two-Year Colleges for Women and Minorities.* Bristol, Pa.: Falmer Press, 1999.

Watson, L. W., and Terrell, M. "Cultural Differences in Student Learning." In F. K. Stage, L. W. Watson, and M. Terrell (eds.), *Enhancing Student Learning: Setting the Campus Context.* Lanham, Md.: University Press of America, 1999.

BARBARA K. TOWNSEND is associate dean for research and development at the University of Missouri-Columbia, where she is also professor of higher education. She is a former community college faculty member and administrator.

*This chapter reports literature from the ERIC system that
highlights issues and concerns regarding minority student
retention and learning success within community colleges.
Factors contributing to declining retention rates and
effective programming strategies designed to address continued participation of students of color are discussed.*

9

Sources and Information Regarding Effective Retention Strategies for Students of Color

Eboni M. Zamani

During the push for educational access and social equity in the 1960s and
1970s, the community college emerged as one of the fastest growing sectors
of American education (Witt, Wattenbarger, Gollattscheck, and Suppiger,
1994). Over the last three decades, institutions of higher learning have wit-
nessed marked increases in minority student enrollment. Demographic projections suggest that greater numbers of students of color will enter the
educational pipeline in the new millennium. As our nation becomes more
diverse, educators and policymakers have the formidable task of not only
attracting students of color to higher education but also ensuring their retention, matriculation, and learning success. Community colleges are often the
primary vehicle of postsecondary opportunities for first-generation, low-
income students and underrepresented racial/ethnic minorities.

    This chapter provides a review of materials pertaining to minority stu-
dent retention and learning success as reflected in the present ERIC database. The present document outlines some of the chief concerns regarding
academic progression and outcomes for community college students of
color. Among those concerns, factors attributed to low minority retention
rates, strategies and programs fostering minority student success, and implications for future research are discussed. Most ERIC documents (publications with ED numbers) can be viewed on microfiche at over nine hundred
libraries worldwide. In addition, most may be ordered on microfiche or on
paper from the ERIC Document Reproduction Service (EDRS) by calling
(800) 443-ERIC. Journal articles are not available from EDRS, but they can

be acquired through regular library channels or purchased from the University Microfilm International Articles Clearinghouse at (800) 521–0600, extension 533.

Factors Related to Retention of Minority College Students

Research addressing retention and attrition suggests that there are numerous factors related to low retention rates of minority college students. Based on a synthesis of issues related to student retention, Upcraft and Gardner (1989) and Upcraft and others (1994) outlined a framework for identifying the student and institutional variables that have an impact on the odds of student success in college: (1) personal characteristics (motivation, previous achievement, and intellectual ability), (2) demographic characteristics (age, gender, and race), (3) cultural characteristics (ethnic background and socioeconomic status), (4) institutional characteristics (campus site, regional location, selectivity, control, curriculum, and enrollment), and (5) institutional climate (student-faculty interaction, student activities, commuter or residential campus). Prior academic achievement and intellectual ability have been considered primary factors affecting student retention and learning success. Among the various student characteristics related to college student attrition, the literature has also noted that students with low-level degree goals, lack of financial resources, poor study habits, full-time employment, and parents with low levels of educational attainment have higher student drop-out rates (Mohammadi, 1994). Other researchers (Belcher, 1992; McGregor, Reece, and Garner, 1997; Rendon, 1995; Smith, 1990) contend that African American, Hispanic, and Native American students often enter college with academic deficiencies (for example, lower grades and test scores) and are underrepresented in four-year institutions—particularly selective colleges and universities—in comparison with white and Asian American students.

Research has indicated institutional characteristics that present challenges in retaining undergraduate students at publicly controlled, less-than-four-year institutions—coeducational, commuter campuses—with large student enrollments and nonselective admissions (Smith, 1990). For African Americans and other underrepresented students of color, poor retention rates reflect a lack of student-college fit. More specifically, success rates for students of color may pale in comparison with those of white students, as the importance of a multicultural curriculum, culturally pluralistic environment, and inclusive campus climate may be lacking at many institutions of higher learning (Haralson, 1996; Smith, 1990). Given the preponderance of students of color attending community colleges, institutional programs and policies designed to enhance learning and to increase minority student retention are needed.

While retention issues are more problematic at community colleges than at four-year institutions, little focus has been given to formulating theoretical models that seek to explain retention and attrition as they relate to students of color (Mohammadi, 1994). Furthermore, few two-year institutions conduct empirical research that seeks to further our understanding of student withdrawal patterns, based on demographic, socioeconomic, and institutional factors.

Although two-year institutions have not commonly conducted institutional research addressing the retention rate of racially/ethnically diverse students, literature in the ERIC database provides some insight regarding the types of studies undertaken by community colleges. Patrick Henry Community College (PHCC) in Virginia conducted a study addressing student retention. Three-fourths of PHCC students were enrolled part-time, nearly two-thirds of the student body were female, and the racial/ethnic composition was 82 percent white, 17 percent African American, and 1 percent other minority. The average age of PHCC students was 28.8, and over 90 percent of the students completing their degree in 1993 indicated that they were employed while attending PHCC (Mohammadi, 1994).

The longitudinal study of PHCC 1988–1989 through 1991–1992 student cohorts revealed that retention rates for white college students were higher than those of African Americans and other minority students. Interestingly, the highest student retention rates were for students identified as other minorities. Overall retention rates were higher among male students in comparison with those of female students. Logistic regression analyses found that the level of students' academic goals, semester hours attempted, total hours completed, semester grade point average, and cumulative grade point average had a significant impact on the odds of student persistence and attainment. The PHCC results were consistent with previous research on college student retention. However, additional analyses illustrated that 40 percent of the Fall 1988 cohort had low retention rates because students had no intention of completing a certificate or degree program (Mohammadi, 1994).

In tracking student progress, the education division of the Washington State Board for Community and Technical Colleges developed a tracking system to monitor community college degree seekers longitudinally. Seppanen (1994) operationally defined substantial student progress as enrollment in Washington state community and technical colleges for four or more quarters during 1991–92. Degree-seeking technical college students were 5 percent less likely than community college students to drop out. Roughly 22 percent of the students who enrolled with the intention of completing a vocational or transfer degree failed to return to college following the first quarter of enrollment. Twenty-nine percent of students made some progress, as indicated by their enrollment for two or three quarters prior to leaving the institution. However, over half of the full-time students and one-third of the part-time students reportedly made substantial progress, in that they enrolled for four or more quarters during the two-year period. Over 49 percent of the students graduated or made substantial progress by persisting toward degree completion. Again consistent with previous research, Seppanen (1994) found that African American and Hispanic degree seekers did not progress to the same extent as other groups of students in pursuit of a degree. However, with the exception of Native American students, there was improvement in the overall progress of students of color, despite higher retention rates for white and Asian American students.

McGregor, Reece, and Garner's report analyzing Fall 1996 course grades for Pima Community College (1997) discussed findings by campus, ethnicity, and age group during the 1981, 1986, 1991, and 1996 fall semesters. More specifically, the researchers operationally defined course grades as successes or withdrawals. Therefore, two categories were used in examining course grades, with successes referring to the grades A, B, C, and P (passing/credit awarded), as opposed to withdrawals, identified by W (official course withdrawal), Y (instructor/general withdrawal), and NC (no credit awarded). Total successes constituted approximately two-thirds of the grades awarded, while the total W and Y grades accounted for one-fourth of all grades awarded. This examination defined and measured learning as the successful completion of courses. In this investigation, grades were found to change over time. Change was attributed to the total number of grades awarded increasing by approximately 25 percent. They suggest that this increase is due to a national trend in which the proportion of A's awarded has escalated. However, literature addressing the learning success of students of color is not exactly replete with percentages parallel to those of majority students, as many more minority students than white students can be accurately described as being at risk or as entering higher education without adequate academic preparation (Boughan, 1996).

In examining grades by ethnicity, McGregor, Reece, and Garner (1997) found that the distribution of grades varied according to group. Their findings corroborate previous studies that illustrate that students of color disproportionately earn fewer A's and B's than do their white counterparts. Specifically, Native American students received the lowest proportion of A's, with African American and Hispanic students receiving lower grades than Asian American and white students. Overall, the study found a decline for Asian American students in the proportion of A's earned. The proportion of A's remained constant for white and Hispanic students while increasing for African American and Native American students, in contrast to previous fall semesters. More important, academic preparedness was not controlled for; therefore the researchers concluded that the distribution of grades may have varied because of prior academic experience, as opposed to race or ethnicity.

The assertions of Harris and Kayes (1996) regarding low retention of minority students being partially attributed to their transition and adjustment into ethnocentric (that is, Eurocentric) college environments are consistent

with what Rendon (1995) describes as the two critical phases affecting retention of first-semester students. First, students of color may have difficulty making the transition to college and making connections in college, once enrolled.
Issues related to transition and adjustment can also be institution-related, as
the campus climate may be perceived as indifferent or not racially inclusive.
Rendon states that phase one is particularly difficult for students who are the
first in their families to attend college. As first-generation students, minorities
are commonly faced with having to navigate multiple identities in order to be
consistently perceived in the same manner among family and old friends,
while establishing themselves in a new educational context. Second, such barriers as poor academic preparation, low socioeconomic status, and the lack of
clear career goals influence minority student retention (Rendon, 1995).

The studies reviewed in this section illustrate that social science and
institutional researchers have made different distinctions in studying student attrition, persistence, retention, and learning success. Adding to the
complexity of accurately reflecting community college student retention and
persistence is the inconsistent tracking of this population. As many students
of color begin their college careers at two-year institutions, the reasons why
many leave these institutions are still not fully understood by educational
researchers and administrators.

Strategies and Programs Fostering Minority Student Success

Community colleges face the institutional dilemma of how to respond to
the lagging retention rates of students of color and promote learning success. Laden (1998) contends that a pivotal way of addressing student retention concerns is by examining the institutional culture and socialization of
a racially and ethnically diverse student population. In other words, student
motivation and achievement are often influenced by the campus climate.
Therefore, students of color are more likely to excel in institutional environments that are culturally diverse, programmatically inclusive, and supportive of multiple approaches to the acquisition of knowledge.

Some colleges and universities have addressed retention disparities by
devising strategies to combat high attrition among this student population.
Initiated in 1981, the Puente Project is one example of organizational
responses to elevate the retention and degree completion rates at two-year
colleges. The Puente Project originated in California to proactively recognize
and remedy the high dropout rate and the low transfer rate of Hispanic community college students, who are often first-generation college students (Laden,
1998). The crux of the program is to bolster the learning success of Hispanic
students by infusing instruction with cultural relevance and by bringing Hispanic students together with Hispanic counselors and mentors who can relate
to their unique experiences. To date, the 38 two-year institutions conducting
the Puente Project serve three thousand new and continuing students each

year. These programs boast 97 percent retention rates, with 48 percent of those completing the Puente Project transferring to four-year colleges and universities (Laden, 1998).

Cazden (1996) conducted a case study of one community college Puente class to gain a better understanding of why the Puente Project has been such a successful collaboration of students, parents, educators, and the community. Each student was paired with a counselor and assigned to a Mexican American mentor who is a college graduate, is a professional in a field closely aligned with the student's own educational and career goals, and is active in the community. In each Puente class, students were given assignments that dealt with their cultural identity and experiences as Mexican Americans. In addition, students were called upon to reflect on their potential to succeed, their educational objectives, and their goals for the future (Cazden, 1996).

As a participant observer, the researcher completed reading and writing assignments that Puente teachers had assigned to all participating students. The mentor assignment was of particular interest to the researcher. Cazden (1996) found that students not only wrote about their mentors but also incorporated their personal experiences. Of the sixteen student assignments thematically coded by the researcher, six topics emerged most frequently: (1) the orientation, (2) the mentor-mentee breakfast, (3) the establishment of the mentor-mentee relationship at the breakfast, (4) the mentor-mentee interactions (mostly by telephone) that occurred between the mentor-mentee breakfast and students' meeting with their mentors at the mentor's workplace, (5) meeting with the mentor at his or her workplace, and (6) the students' reflections. Cazden asserts that there were shared series of events among the Puente students and that the writing assignments placed an emphasis on the use of sensory details, fluency, and confidence-building. However, because the objectives of college composition include expository writing, Puente students were asked to respond more analytically in written assignments. In addition, Cazden (1996) describes how students' educational aspirations and cultural identity were celebrated, validated, and woven into the fabric of the program goals to further their academic, personal, and professional development.

One of the more prominent programs designed to enrich learning success for students attending college is the Student Support Services (SSS) program. As a segment of the Department of Education's TRIO programs, SSS was initiated to provide academic support programs that target first-generation, low-income students as well as students with learning and physical disabilities (Boughan, 1996). Therefore, students of color are often participants, because many are first-generation or low-income college students. Similar to the Puente Project, SSS was designed to address academic development as well as the cultural, emotional, social, and physical concerns of students (Boughan, 1996).

In assessing the academic impact of SSS program participation at Prince George's Community College, a control group comparison approach was used. The three comparison groups were SSS, eligible non-SSS, and all other students. The nonprogram students had similar background characteristics and matched the SSS students with respect to being academically at risk, being a first-generation college student, and having a low-income background (Boughan, 1996). The results indicated that SSS participants in 1996 soundly outperformed the eligible nonparticipant control group, while performing at an equal or slightly higher level than all the other students who were not eligible. For example, twice the number of SSS participants completed degrees or transferred, in contrast with all other students not eligible, and five times as many SSS students as eligible nonparticipants transferred or graduated. However, when examining student performance and persistence by race or ethnicity, 33 percent of white students reached or exceeded 30 credit hours earned, while 25 percent of minority students performed similarly.

Additional analyses were conducted to compare the academic impact of SSS on student academic success with the outcomes of ALANA (African, Latin, Asian, and Native American students) program participants (Boughan, 1996). The ALANA program provides academic support services similar to those of SSS; however, ALANA was specifically designed to meet the needs of at-risk students of color. Selected performance indicators showed that ALANA and SSS appeared to enhance the academic performance of first-time students to the same degree. Roughly 77 percent of ALANA participants had cumulative grade point averages of 2.00 or higher, while 79 percent of those served by SSS achieved comparable cumulative grade point averages. A greater percentage of ALANA students (66 percent) earned 30 credit hours, compared with the SSS participants (51 percent). Finally, SSS students (18.3 percent) and ALANA students (18.5 percent) were equally awarded degrees or transferred to a four-year institution (Boughan, 1996).

Implications for Program Development at Community Colleges

As the college-age population expands, higher education institutions will increasingly face the challenge of meeting the needs of diverse college learners. The literature is saturated with statistics that demonstrate that many racial and ethnic minority students are at a crossroads for achieving learning success and matriculation toward degree completion. Community colleges in particular will be called upon to provide programs that foster the academic development and career goals of students of color, as two-year institutions often serve as the conduit for their academic and professional development.

The research examined here contributes to discerning problematic issues surrounding retaining students of color at two-year institutions. However, assessment of educational outcomes for students of color cannot exclude identifying strategic programming developed to retain minority students. Therefore, community colleges need to be forerunners in recognizing barriers to learning success rather than simply shifting the blame of failure to students. Institutions must facilitate responsive and inclusive learning environments (Harris and Kayes, 1996; Rendon, 1995; Smith, 1990).

Having acknowledged institutional responsibility for disproportionately low retention rates among students of color, Parkland College of Illinois proactively sought funding to improve recruitment and retention of minority students (Harris and Kayes, 1996). Although Parkland has been an active leader in promoting diversity and multicultural education at the two-year college level, real change in the form of decreased minority student attrition had not been achieved. Harris and Kayes (1996) state, "Finally, our efforts are not working because, in spite of all the special programs and allocated resources for minority student achievement, our schools or colleges, our classrooms, are still extremely ethnocentric—since our approaches to teaching, counseling, planning, learning, success, and achievement are based on theories derived from research on middle-class and upper-class, predominantly Eurocentric, male student populations" (p. 9).

Through a Higher Education Cooperation Act (HECA) grant, Parkland College initiated evaluation and assessment of their campus climate in an effort to facilitate greater engagement for minority students, both inside and outside of the classroom environment. In the first year of the HECA grant, Parkland is estimated to have worked with over five hundred administrators, faculty members, and staff members from six community colleges, one private university, three public universities, and a host of K–12 schools. Although the outcomes and full impact of the grant for recruitment and retention of students of color are being determined, Parkland's HECA grant encompassed four interconnected phases: (1) describing and prioritizing characteristics of inclusive educational communities for students of color, (2) designing assessment models for measuring characteristics of inclusive educational communities for students of color, (3) developing strategies and comprehensive institutional plans for inclusion, and 4) developing and implementing all phases of the initiatives in the college.

Students' temporary or permanent withdrawal from two-year institutions can be attributed to myriad factors, including family obligations, employment, finances, and transfer to four-year institutions. Therefore, how we develop and define measures to examine retention is of critical importance to more accurately reflecting and interpreting student attrition.

Based on previous research, community colleges should attempt to restructure their institutional environments in order to encourage self-actualization and matriculation for students of color. In addressing the needs of culturally diverse learners, college educators must continue internal evaluation of existing structures and become more cognizant of the restructuring necessary to create optimal learning conditions for students of color (Kemp, 1990; Rendon, 1995; Rendon and Hope, 1995). In addition, as institutions of higher learning implement programs and services that promote the educational progression of students of color, future research should examine retention beyond an emphasis of observed problems to inquiry that investigates innovative strategies, exemplary programming, and best practices that curb high attrition among two-year college students of color.

References

Belcher, M. J. "College Preparatory Instruction Study Results from Legislative Request." Report. Miami, Fla: Miami-Dade Community College Office of Institutional Research, 1992. (ED 348 112)

Boughan, K. "The Academic Impact of Student Support Services Program Participation in Fiscal Year 1996." Report. Largo, Md.: Prince George's Community College Office of Institutional Research and Analysis, 1996. (ED 423 917)

Cazden, C. B. "The Mentor Paper Writing Assignment in One Community College Puente Class: Preliminary Report from a Participant Observer." Paper presented at Annual Meeting of the American Educational Research Association, New York, 1996. (ED 398 764)

Haralson, M. Jr. "Survival Factors for Black Students on Predominantly White Campuses." Paper presented at Annual Meeting of the National Association of Student Personnel Administrators, Atlanta, Ga., 1996. (ED 402515)

Harris, Z. M., and Kayes, P. "New Statewide Regional Initiative on Creating Inclusive Educational Communities for Minority Students." Paper presented at annual convention of the American Association of Community Colleges, Atlanta, Ga., 1996. (ED 397 891)

Kemp, A. D. "From Matriculation to Graduation: Focusing Beyond Minority Retention." *Journal of Multicultural Counseling and Development*, 1990, *18*, 144–149. (ED 417 930)

Laden, B. V. "An Organizational Response to Welcoming Students of Color." In J. S. Levin (ed.), *Organizational Change in the Community College: A Ripple or a Sea Change?* New Directions for Community Colleges, no. 102. San Francisco: Jossey-Bass, 1998, 31–41. (EJ 569 074)

McGregor, E. N., Reece, D., and Garner, D. "Analysis of Fall 1996 Course Grades." Tucson, Ariz.: Pima Community College Office of Institutional Research, 1997. (ED 413 015)

Mohammadi, J. "Exploring Retention and Attrition in a Two-Year Public Community College." Report. Martinsville, Va.: Patrick Henry Community College Institutional Planning and Research Information Services, 1994. (ED 382 257)

Rendon, L. I. "Facilitating Retention and Transfer for First Generation Students in Community Colleges." Paper presented at the New Mexico Institute, Rural Community College Initiative, Espanola, N. Mex., 1995. (ED 383 369)

Rendon, L. I., and Hope, R. O. *Educating a New Majority: Transforming America's Educational System for Diversity*. San Francisco: Jossey-Bass, 1995. (ED 388 162)

Seppanen, L. "Student Progress—Comparisons Over Time: Washington Community and Technical Colleges, Research Report No. 94–5." Olympia, Wash.: Washington State Board for Community and Technical Colleges Enrollment Planning and Information Services Divisions, 1994. (ED 382 253)

Smith, E. F. "Toward Greater Success for Minority Students on Predominantly White College Campuses." Austin, Tex.: University of Texas, 1990. (ED 333 306)

Upcraft, L. M., and Gardner, J. N. "The Freshman Year Experience. Helping Students Survive and Succeed in College." San Francisco: Jossey-Bass, 1989. (ED310 664)

Upcraft, L. M., and others. *Designing Successful Transitions: A Guide for Orienting Students to College. The Freshman Year Experience*. Monograph series no. 13. Columbia: University of South Carolina, 1994. (ED 368 239)

Witt, A. A., Wattenbarger, J. L., Gollattscheck, J. F., and Suppiger, J. E. "America's Community Colleges: The First Century." Washington, D.C.: American Association of Community Colleges, 1994. (ED 368 415)

EBONI M. ZAMANI is assistant professor of higher education administration at West Virginia University. Her research addresses minority student retention in two- and four-year institutions, affirmative action in higher education, and psychosocial factors affecting student adjustment.

INDEX

Absher, M., 56
Academic failure, risk factors for, 1
Academic self-concept, 14
ACE (American Council on Education), 2, 21, 24
Achievement, effects of teacher expectations on, 36–37
ACPA, 64
African, Latin, Asian, and Native American (ALANA) program, 101
African American students: attitudes and perceptions of, 32; attitudes toward vocational/technical programs, 22; compared to white/Asian students, 96; completion rates of, 58; learning styles of, 39, 78; mentoring, 56; numbers of degree recipients among, 3; progress of, 98; SAT scores of, 8
Agalianos, A., 73, 81
Agosin, M., 67
Alaskan native students, 1, 2
American Association of Community Colleges, 2, 3, 21, 24, 45, 65
American College Testing (ACT), 13–14
American Council on Education (ACE), 2, 21, 24
Arranged Mentor for Instructional Guidance and Organization (or Other) Support (AMIGOS), 59–61
Anderson, J. A., 37, 39
Aptitude-by-interaction (ATI) model, 38
Aragon, S. R., 37, 38, 39, 78
Armstrong, B., 9
Asian American students: attitudes and perceptions of, 32; compared to white and other minority students, 96; demographics/statistics on, 1; enrollment statistics on, 2; mentoring/retention programs for, 57; numbers of degree recipients among, 3; progress of, 98
Asian universities, 88
Assessing Minority Opportunities in Vocational Education project, 21–22
Assessment: of learning styles, 37; of software, 81; of students' needs, 70
Assessment measures: alternative, 12–15; of outcomes of Middlesex Community

College student diversity program, 70; student portfolios as, 14–15; value-added, 15
Astin, A., 10, 14, 45, 48
Attrition, student characteristics related to, 96
Avalos, J., 10, 14

Bales, F., 87
Bamburg, J. D., 36
Barefoot, B. O., 46, 47, 48, 49, 50, 51, 52
Barnes, R., 9
Barnett, B. G., 12, 13
Basic Academic Subjects Examination (BASE), 10–11
Bates College, 11
Beal, P., 46
Bean, J. P., 45
Beatty-Guenter, P., 57
Beaudry, J., 78
Belcher, M. J., 46, 96
Bicultural awareness, 88
Bigelow, B., 81
Black students. *See* African American students
Boughan, K., 98, 100, 101
Boutte, G. S., 78
Boverie, P., 78
Bowdoin College, 11
Boyer, P., 23
Brawer, F. B., 20
Briscoe, D. B., 4
Brookfield, S. D., 3
Brown, J. S., 37
Bruder, I., 75
Budgeting for student activities, 67

Career development, 49
Carlson, S., 10
Carnegie Foundation, 23
Cazden, C. B., 100
Center for Organizational Problem Enlightenment (COPE), 60
Chao, G. T., 59
Cheng, L. L., 3
Chenoweth, K., 8, 9, 10
Chicano students, 32
Chickering, A. W., 88, 89

Back Issue/Subscription Order Form

Copy or detach and send to:
Jossey-Bass Inc., 350 Sansome Street, San Francisco CA 94104-1342

Call or fax toll free!
Phone 888-378-2537 6AM-5PM PST; Fax 800-605-2665

Back issues: Please send me the following issues at $25 each
(Important: please include series initials and issue number, such as CC90)

1. CC _____

_____

$ _____ Total for single issues

$ _____ Shipping charges (for single issues *only;* subscriptions are exempt
from shipping charges): Up to $30, add $5^{50} • $30^{01}–$50, add $6^{50}
$50^{01}–$75, add $8 • $75^{01}–$100, add $10 • $100^{01}–$150, add $12
Over $150, call for shipping charge

Subscriptions Please ❑ start ❑ renew my subscription to *New Directions
for Community Colleges* for the year ___ at the following rate:

U.S.:	❑ Individual $60	❑ Institutional $107
Canada:	❑ Individual $85	❑ Institutional $132
All Others:	❑ Individual $90	❑ Institutional $137

NOTE: Subscriptions are quarterly, and are for the calendar year only.
Subscriptions begin with the Spring issue of the year indicated above.

$ _____ Total single issues and subscriptions (Add appropriate sales tax for
your state for single issue orders. No sales tax for U.S. subscriptions.
Canadian residents, add GST for subscriptions and single issues.)

❑ Payment enclosed (U.S. check or money order only)

❑ VISA, MC, AmEx, Discover Card #_____ Exp. date_____

Signature _____ Day phone _____

❑ Bill me (U.S. institutional orders only. Purchase order required)

Purchase order #_____

Federal Tax ID 13559 3032   GST 89102-8052

Name _____

Address _____

_____

Phone_____ E-mail _____

For more information about Jossey-Bass, visit our Web site at:
www.josseybass.com   **PRIORITY CODE = ND1**

United States Postal Service

Statement of Ownership, Management, and Circulation

1. Publication Title	2. Publication Number	3. Filing Date
New Directions For Community Colleges	0 1 9 4 – 3 0 8 1	9/29/00

4. Issue Frequency	5. Number of Issues Published Annually	6. Annual Subscription Price
Quarterly	4	$63.00 Individual $115.00 Institution

7. Complete Mailing Address of Known Office of Publication *(Not printer) (Street, city, county, state, and ZIP+4)*
350 Sansome Street
San Francisco, CA 94104
(San Francisco County)

Contact Person
Joe Schuman
Telephone
415-782-3232

8. Complete Mailing Address of Headquarters or General Business Office of Publisher *(Not printer)*
Same As Above

9. Full Names and Complete Mailing Addresses of Publisher, Editor, and Managing Editor *(Do not leave blank)*

Publisher *(Name and complete mailing address)*
Jossey-Bass, A Wiley Company
(Above Address)

Editor *(Name and complete mailing address)*
Arthur M. Cohen
Eric Clearinghouse For Community Clgs-Univ. Of Ca
3051 Moore Hall Box 95121
Los Angeles, CA 90095-1521

Managing Editor *(Name and complete mailing address)*
None

10. Owner *(Do not leave blank. If the publication is owned by a corporation, give the name and address of the corporation immediately followed by the names and addresses of all stockholders owning or holding 1 percent or more of the total amount of stock. If not owned by a corporation, give the names and addresses of the individual owners. If owned by a partnership or other unincorporated firm, give its name and address as well as those of each individual owner. If the publication is published by a nonprofit organization, give its name and address.)*

Full Name	Complete Mailing Address
John Wiley & Sons Inc.	605 Third Avenue New York, NY 10158-0012

11. Known Bondholders, Mortgagees, and Other Security Holders Owning or Holding 1 Percent or More of Total Amount of Bonds, Mortgages, or Other Securities. If none, check box → ☐ None

Full Name	Complete Mailing Address
Same As Above	Same As Above

12. Tax Status *(For completion by nonprofit organizations authorized to mail at nonprofit rates) (Check one)*
The purpose, function, and nonprofit status of this organization and the exempt status for federal income tax purposes:
☐ Has Not Changed During Preceding 12 Months
☐ Has Changed During Preceding 12 Months *(Publisher must submit explanation of change with this statement)*

PS Form **3526**, October 1999   *(See Instructions on Reverse)*

---

13. Publication Title	14. Issue Date for Circulation Data Below
New Directions For Community Colleges	Summer 2000

15.		Extent and Nature of Circulation	Average No. Copies Each Issue During Preceding 12 Months	No. Copies of Single Issue Published Nearest to Filing Date
a.		Total Number of Copies *(Net press run)*	1,919	2,512
b. Paid and/or Requested Circulation	(1)	Paid/Requested Outside-County Mail Subscriptions Stated on Form 3541. *(Include advertiser's proof and exchange copies)*	806	801
	(2)	Paid In-County Subscriptions Stated on Form 3541 *(Include advertiser's proof and exchange copies)*	0	0
	(3)	Sales Through Dealers and Carriers, Street Vendors, Counter Sales, and Other Non-USPS Paid Distribution	0	0
	(4)	Other Classes Mailed Through the USPS	0	0
c.		Total Paid and/or Requested Circulation *[Sum of 15b. (1), (2),(3),and (4)]* ▶	806	801
d. Free Distribution by Mail (Samples, complimentary, and other free)	(1)	Outside-County as Stated on Form 3541	1	1
	(2)	In-County as Stated on Form 3541	0	0
	(3)	Other Classes Mailed Through the USPS	0	0
e.		Free Distribution Outside the Mail *(Carriers or other means)*	156	157
f.		Total Free Distribution *(Sum of 15d. and 15e.)* ▶	157	158
g.		Total Distribution *(Sum of 15c. and 15f)* ▶	963	959
h.		Copies not Distributed	956	1,553
i.		Total *(Sum of 15g. and h.)* ▶	1,919	2,571
j.		Percent Paid and/or Requested Circulation *(15c. divided by 15g. times 100)*	84%	84%

16. Publication of Statement of Ownership
☒ Publication required. Will be printed in the Winter 2000 issue of this publication.   ☐ Publication not required.

17. Signature and Title of Editor, Publisher, Business Manager, or Owner
Susan E. Lewis   Vice President&Publisher/Periodicals   Date 9/29/00

(signature) Susan E. Lewis

I certify that all information furnished on this form is true and complete. I understand that anyone who furnishes false or misleading information on this form or who omits material or information requested on the form may be subject to criminal sanctions (including fines and imprisonment) and/or civil sanctions (including civil penalties).

Instructions to Publishers

1. Complete and file one copy of this form with your postmaster annually on or before October 1. Keep a copy of the completed form for your records.

2. In cases where the stockholder or security holder is a trustee, include in items 10 and 11 the name of the person or corporation for whom the trustee is acting. Also include the names and addresses of individuals who are stockholders who own or hold 1 percent or more of the total amount of bonds, mortgages, or other securities of the publishing corporation. In item 11, if none, check the box. Use blank sheets if more space is required.

3. Be sure to furnish all circulation information called for in item 15. Free circulation must be shown in items 15d, e, and f.

4. Item 15h., Copies not Distributed, must include (1) newsstand copies originally stated on Form 3541, and returned to the publisher, (2) estimated returns from news agents, and (3), copies for office use, leftovers, spoiled, and all other copies not distributed.

5. If the publication had Periodicals authorization as a general or requester publication, this Statement of Ownership, Management, and Circulation must be published; it must be printed in any issue in October or, if the publication is not published during October, the first issue printed after October.

6. In item 16, indicate the date of the issue in which this Statement of Ownership will be published.

7. Item 17 must be signed.

Failure to file or publish a statement of ownership may lead to suspension of Periodicals authorization.

PS Form **3526**, October 1999 *(Reverse)*